SHOPPING NUTRITION

THE DAIRY CASE

Your surest source of calcium

Whole Milk · 2% Milk
Skim Milk · Buttermilk

Everyone needs
2 cups of milk each day.
Kids and mothers need more.

MILK PRODUCTS

Cottage Cheese
Cream Cheese
Natural and
Processed Cheese
Yogurt
Ice Cream

MONEY $AVING $PECIALS

Nonfat Dry Milk
Evaporated Milk

...ternate
...otein
...urces

Peas
Beans
ls
uts, Peanut Butter

Butter
Margarine
Vegetable Oil — *(high in polyunsaturates)*

BREADS, CEREALS, FLOUR, MIXES

For best value, choose whole grain, enriched or restored. Read the label.

Bread and Rolls
Cooked Cereal
Cornmeal
Crackers
Flour
Ready-to-eat Cereal

SAVE SWEETS
for
TREATS

Grits
Macaroni
Spaghetti
Noodles
Rice
Rolled Oats

FARM JOURNAL'S
HOMEMADE SNACKS

FARM JOURNAL'S

HOMEMADE SNACKS

How to Eat Better When You Eat on the Run

By Nell B. Nichols
FARM JOURNAL Field Food Editor

Doubleday & Company, Inc.
Garden City, New York

Library of Congress Cataloging in Publication Data

Nichols, Nell Beaubien.
    Farm journal's homemade snacks.

    Includes index.
    1. Snack foods.   I. Farm journal (Philadelphia,
1956–   )   II. Title.
TX740.N5   641.5′63
ISBN 0-385-12307-8
Library of Congress Catalog Card Number 76–10063

CONTENTS

Acknowledgments ix

Introduction   SNACK YOUR WAY TO HEALTH   1

Chapter 1   NIBBLES THAT NOURISH   9

Chapter 2   SNACK BUT STAY SLIM   21

Chapter 3   CAPITALIZE ON FRUITS AND
            VEGETABLES   41

Chapter 4   BREADS WITH A HEALTH BONUS   63

Chapter 5   MILK . . . STILL THE DEPENDABLE   91

Chapter 6   SUBSTANTIAL SNACKS FOR MEAL-
            MISSERS   109

Chapter 7   SWEETS TO EAT WITH A BETTER
            CONSCIENCE   137

Chapter 8   MAKE SNACKS COUNT IN THE DAY'S
            MEALS   165

Chapter 9   GROCERY SHOPPING FOR GOOD
            NUTRITION   177

Index   197

ACKNOWLEDGMENTS

The idea for this book grew out of conversations over the years with Betsy McCracken, home economist specializing in food—and mother of my four grandchildren. Betsy and I have long been convinced of the need for a book on how to make snacks or off-hour mini-meals a healthier part of the day's eating. Her convictions developed while cooking for her husband, daughter and three sons, all with busy schedules at work or school.

The best thing a mother can do, Betsy feels, is to have the "right" foods easily available when the children get home, or when everyone wants something to munch on while watching TV. As we went to work on the book, it was Betsy's job not only to test and develop the recipes and serving ideas, but also to prove them practical under home conditions. To us, this means that shopping for these extra mini-meals and their preparation should fit easily into normal homemaking and meal planning routine. And—even more important—family members should enjoy the snacks and choose to eat them.

Nutritionists are emphasizing the "planned snack" as a way to work essential food value into these casual bites between meals. Early in the preparation of this book, we met with Dr. Ruth M. Leverton, for many years the Science Advisor on Food and Nutrition for the U. S. Department of Agriculture. She is the author of *Food Becomes You* (published by Iowa State University Press; now available in paperback from Dolphin Books), and of many articles on nutrition and eating for good health. Dr. Leverton prepared the material in Chapter 9, "Grocery Shopping for Good Nutrition," which is a practical, everyday approach to healthful eating. Serving as our nutrition consultant, she also carefully reviewed the entire manuscript.

Two FARM JOURNAL editors also helped shape this book. Gertrude Dieken encouraged me in the planning and direction; Kathryn Larson worked with all of us to verify facts and put the book in order.

FARM JOURNAL'S

HOMEMADE SNACKS

Introduction

SNACK YOUR WAY
TO HEALTH

You may think of snacks as food you eat at coffee time, what your husband and children nibble on evenings while watching television, or as something to share with guests. And everybody knows snacks are what hungry children hurry to the kitchen for when they get home from school. They are all these things and even at times a mini-meal that takes the place of a complete meal around the family table. Young people delayed at the dinner hour by school activities and jobs must depend on off-hour meals.

A break in the day—for extra nourishment and for enjoyment —is basically a good concept. But like every good idea, it can be carried too far, or can be abused.

Eating between meals has always been part of American life. Pioneer women called it "piecing" except when there was company—then it became "refreshments." Through the 1930s, any active child or hardworking farmer could burn up thousands of calories a day; piecing was the way to get enough calories to keep going.

Now with machines doing so much of our work and burning energy for us, we no longer need as many between-meal calories. But we haven't given up (and likely won't) the long-established and pleasant habit of eating at other than three mealtimes.

Today more than ever, this fits our lifestyle. We associate snacks with fun and good times. A hospitable bite to eat is part of our happiness at being with friends, part of our enjoyment of leisure time with our families . . . the doughnuts we dunk during midmorning coffee breaks, the popcorn and other crunchies we nibble on while watching TV, the soft drinks we take from the coin machines at the gas station, the cookies the children wolf down after school, the desserts we serve after a club meeting or an evening of cards.

More and more, the kinds of food we munch on are crowding out or even substituting for regular meals. Many teen-agers eat on the run, between school and band practice or part-time jobs. Office workers use lunch hours to run errands; mothers at home nibble instead of taking time to fix a real lunch. Some of us nibble too much, sometimes out of boredom or frustration.

In these ways, we carelessly lose count of the servings of essential foods we should be getting, our appetites lulled by satisfying our hunger absentmindedly. Most of us will join with nutritionists in regretting that many Americans are overweight and undernourished at the same time, not because the food isn't available but because we choose unwisely the foods we eat.

This may not be true of your family. Certainly the fact that you're reading this book about "healthier snacking" shows your concern about what your family eats. But unfortunately, packaged snacks are in the picture for most Americans. Every ten years the U.S. government takes a *Household Food Consumption Survey* and the comparison of figures from one decade to the next shows that consumption of the popular snack foods is rising faster than the population growth would warrant.

As such studies suggest, in-between-meal eating is likely to increase rather than diminish. And wise parents might well heed the advice, "If you can't lick 'em, join 'em." It will be easier for you to change your family's snacks than to change their habit of snacking.

HOW TO MAKE SNACKS COUNT

The new idea that snacks can be excellent carriers of nutrients for the whole family's well-being is the reason for this book. Why not, we reasoned, face the facts and make snacks a part of the day's nutrition? Why not make such popular snack foods as cookies and bread more nutritious? Why not discard some old notions about what's proper to eat or serve for breakfast or supper or some special occasion? Why not make some snacks good enough to take the place of meals?

That is exactly what we have done in developing recipes for HOMEMADE SNACKS. We suggest these mini-meals and in-between-meal treats to offer you the opportunity to make everything your family eats count toward good health.

Over the years we have developed a fixed pattern for feeding our families—three square meals a day that aren't complete without a dessert, for example. Or we insist that a hearty breakfast is essential, when actually a light breakfast might be better if you were snacking late the evening before.

When you cut yourself loose from set meal patterns, you'll want some new guidelines. In Chapter 8, we show you how to "Make Snacks Count in the Day's Meals"—how to select them to supply vitamins, minerals and possibly protein, *in addition* to energy. We also include some suggestions for making entire meals—acceptably nutritious—out of snack foods.

You don't have to be a nutritionist to choose snacks that will round out your day's menus. In Chapter 9, "Grocery Shopping for Good Nutrition," Dr. Ruth M. Leverton, our consultant on nutrition, describes the different foods your family needs to eat each day; you'll see this information in chart form inside the front and back covers of this book. It will make snack planning more interesting and helpful for you and the family.

The introductions to each of the recipe chapters also spell out the role snacks can play as meal supplements. There are more than 200 recipes for snacks in this book. All of them are tasty foods that contain necessary nutrients. Some of them also supply roughage or fiber which is often missing in our modern diets; fiber foods help the intestinal tract to function properly and in healthy condition. Not one of the snacks is filled with only "empty calories."

HELPING CHILDREN DEVELOP GOOD EATING HABITS

To give homemade snacks the best chance to help with nutrition for health requires the commitment of both mothers and fathers. Often when family food habits are discussed, parents feel guilty. Either they know they should be doing something to improve them and aren't . . . or they feel they can't meet the competition from the ready-made snacks that saturate their children's world.

Eating habits have to be taught to each generation, just like brushing teeth or learning the multiplication tables or the alphabet. Children get their food habits and much of their attitude toward healthful eating from parents, just as they do their personal hygiene. Some nutrition is taught in schools, but by the time the child gets to school his food habits are pretty well formed. Schools can reinforce good habits but it's often too late to correct bad ones. Those early years are so important!

Any food you provide leaves an impression. Snacks can fill in gaps for both spot hunger and nutritional needs. They have tremendous potential in terms of nutrition and health. Here are a few suggestions on how to handle snacking:

Start preschool children on healthy snacks. If they learn to like healthful foods, they are likely to enjoy them throughout life.

Go slow in describing the merits of different snacks. Keep some appetizing nutritious foods available and let them sell themselves. What do your children find when they open the refrigerator? A pitcher of fruit juice is an invitation to pour a glassful rather than open a sugar-laden carbonated beverage. A bowl of oatmeal-raisin cookie dough suggests to the older children baking a batch of cookies. In the freezer, individual-size snacks, such as sandwiches, pizzas, soups and little casseroles ready to heat encourage older children and grownups to eat good mini-meals.

Keep a covered jar of mixed vegetable or fruit salad in the refrigerator to tempt snackers to help themselves. Such chilled mixtures are an excellent way to include vegetables, rich in vitamins and minerals and often slighted, in snack menus. It is easy to spoon out a serving to eat with a sandwich.

Make and refrigerate a cheese sandwich or two or some cup custard. You may be surprised to find that the youngster too hurried to eat breakfast will grab the sandwich to eat in the bus on the way to school and he'll get his protein that way. Or he may take time to eat the custard before leaving. Custard will give him the same protein he refuses in a scrambled egg.

Plan some oversize meals that will provide leftovers to save for snacks. Hungry teen-agers will welcome a piece of sweet potato pie, oatmeal cake or the remnants of a meat loaf to use in making a sandwich; all these will hold in the refrigerator.

Many people not only like to have a part in selecting their snacks, but they also like to fix them, or at least help in getting them ready. It's an especially good idea to let little children take some responsibility for their snacks. Suggest that they spread the slice of bread with peanut butter or a sandwich spread. Give them milk or fruit juice in a small pitcher so they can pour their own. Teaching youngsters to participate in the preparation of their snacks is excellent training that gives them interest in foods. It is an up-to-date way to get their cooperation in the kitchen—and in the diet.

WHAT MAKES A GOOD SNACK?

A good snack should consist of a solid food and a liquid. When a person feels exhausted at four o'clock in the afternoon, nutritionists say it could be simply dehydration. Even a glass of water is a wonderful pickup—and no calories! Or you can pour a glass of tomato juice or fruit juice and benefit from the nutrients in them. The solid food should contribute some of the nutrients in short supply in the food-day.

Many parents could do a better job in selecting the snacks they eat themselves. Busy mothers who are alone at noon frequently settle for a cup of coffee or tea. Their refusal of food may spring from the wish to lose a few pounds, but this can be at the expense of energy and general health (and sets a poor example for children).

Men sometimes snack the evening through on cereal-nut mixes, never thinking they are overeating. If they eat a substantial snack at bedtime, they cannot expect to have much appetite for a healthful breakfast the next morning. People of all ages can eat and drink happily on the nutritious low-calorie recipes included in this book, or on small servings of snacks that contain more calories.

Do watch the *size* of these servings. The amount of food required between meals depends to a large extent on the age and activity of the snacker. Many preschool children need a bit of food to tide them over from one meal to the next. But, since growth slows down after the second birthday, a small serving is all that's necessary. This might be a graham cracker and a small glass of orange juice. Permitting children to eat larger servings than they need is a sure way to create food and health problems. It may even start them on the road to obesity.

Older youngsters—from ten to twelve years through the twenty-first or twenty-second year—grow rapidly not only in weight and height but in bone density and in the development of stronger muscles. They need larger quantities of food. Some teen-agers, especially boys, can eat a hearty after-school snack and still need and enjoy a full-size evening meal.

As adults approach middle age, their eating habits, if not modified, often lead to overweight. This is the modern problem in nutrition: to get all the nutrients the body needs without also getting too many calories. Because Americans today are not as physically active as they used to be, and become less so in later life, the Recommended Daily Allowance (RDA) of calories has been reduced from formerly recommended levels. This is why nutritionists now emphasize the "nutrient density" of foods. Here's what it means:

Four ounces of fruit-flavored drink and four ounces of orange juice have almost the same calorie count. Both meet the RDA for vitamin C. But the orange juice also contributes bits of other nutrients such as protein, calcium, iron, vitamin A, thiamin, potassium, folic acid and vitamin B_6. Not much of each—but if you keep a close tab on calories, every nutrient bit counts. Even with its extra nutrients, the orange juice is actually slightly less caloric than most fruit drinks.

This idea of nutrient density has been our guide in developing recipes for this book. This is why, in Chapter 9, we emphasize the need for *variety* in the diet. You may wonder whether a half cup of wheat germ or raisins in a batch of cookies is going to make much difference. But if you're going to eat cookies anyway —and take in the calories—why not also absorb extra little bits of vitamins and minerals?

By making your own snacks, you will have exact knowledge of the healthful ingredients in them. Depending on the food provided in menus for the rest of the day, you will know which kinds of foods to place front and center on the counter or in the refrigerator for your snacking family to help themselves.

The recipe chapters are arranged according to such food needs. For example, there's a chapter featuring milk and milk products, another on fruits and vegetables. Cereal grains show up in nourishing nibbles in Chapter 1, and also in the recipes for breads, and for cookies and cakes in the Sweets chapter. We've included a chapter on low-calorie snacking, and one featuring snacks hearty enough to serve as meals for someone in a hurry. Chapter introductions have more suggestions for making everything you eat a beneficial part of your day's intake. As you fit these ideas into your routine, the rewards will be great in terms of your health and your family's.

Chapter 1

NIBBLES THAT NOURISH

Finger foods your husband and children are likely to nibble on evenings while watching television, reading or relaxing can wreck your plans to feed your family well if they add unneeded calories or calories without nutrients. But the right finger foods could actually be a help to good nutrition; they can take on great responsibility for furnishing essential nutrients to the daily diet and ease the load on regular meals.

Foods that adapt themselves to making or assembling some tasty, nutritious snacks for nibbling are:

> Whole-grain and fortified cereals
> Nuts and peanuts
> Sunflower and sesame seeds
> Dried fruits, particularly raisins

All the recipes in this chapter focus on these foods which supply essential nutrients. They do not necessarily produce low-calorie specials—for those, see the next chapter.

Whole grain and fortified cereals are important sources of energy from their starch, plus several B-vitamins, iron and other minerals. Another asset is the fiber in whole grain cereals. Cereals can also be an important source of protein although this value is often overlooked.

Nuts and peanuts furnish protein, B-vitamins, iron and other minerals and considerable fat. Most of our recipes for finger foods combine a comparatively small amount of nuts with a larger quantity of crisp cereals. The result is a pleasing variety in both texture and flavor.

Cereal Snack Mix, for example, contains one cup of peanuts to six cups of three kinds of cereals. In some recipes, such as Peanut Cereal Bars and Double Peanut Popcorn Balls, peanut butter provides fat and adds flavor and valuable nutrients.

Sunflower seeds are an "in" food with many young people, and have about the same nutrients as nuts. With Honey Nut Butter, composed of peanuts, sunflower and sesame seeds, you create a jackpot of flavor and good nutrition.

Dried fruits not only contribute sweetness but also iron and several other minerals, including potassium. Four dried fruits team with crunchy granola cereal in luscious Date Coconut Balls. The recipe for Golden Apricot Logs won a place in this collection of good-tasting, nutritious finger foods.

You realize that good ingredients to make good snacks will show up on your food budget. But if you compare what you have made with some of the highly advertised "junk foods," you will be proud of the way your snacks score.

CEREAL SNACK MIX

Perfect choice for nibblers who should eat unsweetened snacks

½ c. butter or margarine
1 to 2 tblsp. Worcestershire sauce
½ tsp. seasoned salt
¼ tsp. garlic salt
¼ tsp. onion salt
2 c. bite-size shredded wheat squares
2 c. bite-size shredded corn squares
2 c. bite-size shredded rice squares
2 c. thin pretzel sticks
1 c. dry roasted peanuts or soy nuts

In small saucepan melt butter; stir in seasonings.

In large mixing bowl, combine remaining ingredients. Pour on butter mixture and toss gently to distribute. Spread evenly in a 13×9×2″ pan.

Bake in 325° oven for 20 minutes, stirring several times. Makes about 2½ quarts.

POPCORN CEREAL CRUNCH

Crisp texture, superlative flavor win top rating for this snack

8 c. popped corn (about ⅓ c. unpopped)

2 c. bite-size shredded wheat squares

1 c. blanched whole almonds, toasted

1½ c. sugar

1 c. light corn syrup

½ c. butter or margarine

1 tsp. vanilla

¼ tsp. ground cinnamon

Combine popped corn, shredded wheat cereal and almonds in greased Dutch oven. Keep warm in 250° oven.

Combine sugar, corn syrup and butter in medium saucepan. Cook over medium heat, stirring constantly, until mixture comes to a boil. Continue cooking without stirring until temperature reaches 290° on candy thermometer (soft-crack stage). Remove from heat; stir in vanilla and cinnamon.

Pour slowly over popped corn mixture, stirring constantly until mixture is well coated. Spread immediately on 2 greased baking sheets. Cool; break in pieces. Store in tightly covered container. Makes about 2 pounds.

PEANUT CEREAL SNACK MIX

Sweetened cereal eliminates need for more sugar

4 c. sweet shredded oat
  cereal
1 c. dry roasted peanuts

¼ c. butter or margarine
2 tblsp. peanut butter
¼ tsp. ground cinnamon

In bowl combine cereal and peanuts. Melt butter and peanut butter over low heat; blend in cinnamon. Pour butter mixture over cereal and toss to coat evenly. Spread in 15×10×1" jelly roll pan. Heat in 350° oven 10 to 12 minutes, stirring once or twice. Makes 5 cups.

PEPPY POPCORN

Popcorn and potatoes are energy foods; nuts and cheese add protein. A crisp, flavorful snack on the salty side

8 c. popped corn (about ⅓
  c. unpopped)
1 (1½ oz.) can shoestring
  potatoes (1½ c.)
1 (7 oz.) jar dry roasted
  mixed nuts
½ c. grated Parmesan
  cheese

⅓ c. butter or margarine,
  melted
½ tsp. chili powder
½ tsp. garlic salt
½ tsp. onion salt

Combine popcorn, potatoes, nuts and cheese. Stir together butter and seasonings. Pour over popcorn mixture. Toss to mix. Makes 11 cups.

COUNTRY-STYLE GRANOLA

Put a bowl of this healthful mix on the coffee table and watch family and guests enjoy its flavor and crispness

5 c. old-fashioned rolled
  oats
1½ c. wheat germ
1 c. shredded coconut
1 c. chopped peanuts
½ c. whole wheat bran

½ c. brown sugar, firmly
  packed
½ c. vegetable oil
⅓ c. water
2 tsp. vanilla

Stir together oats, wheat germ, coconut, peanuts, wheat bran and brown sugar.

Combine oil, water and vanilla; pour over cereal mixture and mix thoroughly. Turn into 15×10×1″ pan, or other large, shallow pan. Bake in 350° oven 1 hour, stirring every 15 minutes. Cool and store in tightly covered container. Makes about 10 cups.

FIVE-CUP SNACK MIX

Coconut and raisins add just the right touch of sweetness

1 c. shredded coconut
1 c. roasted peanuts
1 c. roasted cashews

1 c. sunflower seeds
1 c. raisins

Place coconut in shallow pan. Bake in 350° oven until toasted, about 15 minutes. Stir occasionally. Combine with remaining ingredients. Makes 5 cups.

SPICY NUTS

Simply great to nibble on during the card game

¼ c. cooking oil
1½ tsp. chili powder
½ tsp. cayenne pepper
½ tsp. garlic salt
1 tsp. Worcestershire sauce

1 (7 oz.) jar dry roasted
  cashews (1½ c.)
1 (8 oz.) jar dry roasted
  peanuts (1½ c.)

In mixing bowl combine oil and seasonings. Add cashews and peanuts; toss to coat. Spread evenly in 13×9×2″ pan. Place in 300° oven for 20 minutes, stirring once or twice. Makes 3 cups.

HONEY NUT BUTTER

Spread on hot breakfast toast for a day's healthy start. For a change, add ⅓ cup raisins with other ingredients

3 tblsp. vegetable oil
3 tblsp. honey
½ c. roasted salted peanuts

¼ c. roasted salted
  sunflower seeds
¼ c. sesame seeds

Place all ingredients in blender container. Blend at high speed until smooth, stopping blender frequently to scrape down sides. Makes about ¾ cup.

FRUIT NUT BALLS

A sweet worth its calories in minerals and vitamins

1 c. pitted prunes	½ tsp. salt
1 c. pitted dates	2 tblsp. honey
1 c. dark raisins	2 tblsp. orange juice
1 c. light raisins	1 tsp. grated orange peel
1 c. shredded coconut	1 c. finely chopped nuts
½ c. wheat germ	

Put prunes, dates, raisins and coconut through food chopper, using fine blade. Knead in wheat germ, salt, honey, orange juice and orange peel.

(The amount of moisture in dried fruits varies. If mixture is sticky, knead in a little more wheat germ. If mixture is too dry, add a small amount of orange juice.)

Form into 1″ balls. Roll in nuts. Cover tightly and store in refrigerator up to 1 month. Makes about 4 dozen balls.

DOUBLE PEANUT POPCORN BALLS

More delicious, less crisp and easier to eat than most popcorn balls. Great selection for children's holiday refreshments

5 c. popped corn	½ c. chunk-style peanut
1 c. roasted peanuts	butter
½ c. sugar	½ tsp. vanilla
½ c. light corn syrup	

Lightly salt popped corn, add peanuts and keep warm in 225° oven.

Combine sugar and corn syrup in small saucepan. Cook over medium heat, stirring constantly, just until mixture comes to a full rolling boil. Remove from heat and stir in peanut butter and vanilla. Immediately pour over popcorn and peanuts; mix well. With buttered hands, form mixture into balls, using ½ c. mixture for each ball. Makes 10 balls.

PEANUT COCOA-CEREAL BARS

This confection is a stand-in for candy enjoyed by all ages

1 c. chunk-style peanut butter

2 tblsp. butter or margarine, softened

1¼ c. sifted confectioners sugar

3 c. chocolate flavor corn puffs

1 c. coarsely chopped peanuts

Line a square 8″ pan with aluminum foil, bringing foil up over pan edges.

Blend together peanut butter, butter and confectioners sugar. With hands mix in cereal, crushing it slightly. Press into pan. Sprinkle with peanuts and press in firmly. Chill several hours.

To serve, pull up foil to remove confection from pan. Cut in 1×1½″ bars. Makes 4 dozen.

CORN NUT TOFFEE

Carmelized sugar enhances taste of this special sweet

1 c. butter or margarine

1 c. sugar

2 c. puffed corn cereal

½ c. broken pecans

Melt butter over low heat in large, heavy skillet. Add sugar and cook, stirring constantly, until mixture becomes light brown and thickens. Remove at once from heat. Stir in cereal and pecans. Turn out on ungreased baking sheet; quickly spread ¼″ thick, or to cover an area about 12×10″. Cool; break into pieces. Makes about 4 dozen.

PEANUT CEREAL BAR COOKIES

These tasty, no-bake cookies take little time or effort

1 c. sugar
1 c. light corn syrup
1 c. peanut butter

6 c. high-protein cereal flakes

Combine sugar and corn syrup in saucepan. Cook and stir over medium heat until mixture comes to a boil. Boil 1 minute. Remove from heat and add peanut butter, stirring until well blended. Pour over cereal. Toss to coat evenly. Spread in buttered 13×9×2″ pan. Cool. Cut in 2×1½″ bars. Makes 3 dozen.

DATE COCONUT BALLS

Sweet without sugar! Nuts and granola add slight crunchiness

½ c. butter or margarine
1 (8 oz.) pkg. pitted
    chopped dates
¼ tsp. ground cinnamon

¾ c. chopped pecans
¾ c. plain granola cereal
¾ c. shredded coconut

In heavy saucepan combine butter, dates and cinnamon. Cook over low heat, stirring constantly, until butter is melted and blended thoroughly with dates. Chill until mixture is firm enough to be molded and hold its shape. Stir in pecans and granola. Form tablespoonfuls of mixture into balls. Roll in coconut to coat thoroughly. Makes about 2½ dozen.

CASSEROLE DATE COOKIES

Shape these confections after baking. For a change use ¾ cup chopped dates and ¼ cup chopped dried apricots

2 eggs	**1 c. chopped nuts**
1 c. sugar	**1 c. flaked coconut**
Dash of salt	**1 tsp. vanilla**
1 c. finely chopped dates	**Sugar**

Beat eggs well. Gradually add sugar, beating until mixture is fluffy. Add salt. Fold in dates, nuts, coconut and vanilla. Pour into greased 2-quart casserole.

Bake, uncovered, in 350° oven 30 minutes. (Center of mixture may not appear baked.)

Remove from oven and stir with wooden spoon to mix; let stand until cool enough to handle. Shape in small balls; roll in sugar. Store in covered container. If cookie balls become too soft, roll in more sugar. Makes 27 to 30 cookies.

GOLDEN APRICOT LOGS

Holiday favorite from a California fruit grower's wife

1 c. dried apricots	**1 tblsp. orange juice**
⅓ c. flaked coconut	**½ c. flaked coconut**
¼ tsp. grated orange peel	

If apricots are moist packed, put through food chopper, using finest blade. If apricots are not moist, first put them in a sieve and steam them over simmering water 5 minutes.

Combine ground apricots with ⅓ c. coconut and put through food chopper again. Thoroughly mix in orange peel and juice. Divide mixture in half, wrap separately and chill thoroughly.

On a board, roll half the mixture with your hands to make a log about 6″ long. Sprinkle ¼ c. coconut on board and continue rolling apricot mixture in coconut until 12″ long. Cut in 1″ pieces. Repeat with other half. Makes 2 dozen.

CARAMEL CHOCOLATE APPLES

Peanuts add protein, iron and B-vitamins to apple treat

6 medium red apples
½ c. chopped peanuts
1 (14 oz.) pkg. caramels

¼ c. semisweet chocolate
   pieces
2 tblsp. hot water

Wash and dry apples. Stick a wooden skewer in stem end of each. Divide peanuts in 6 equal-size mounds on waxed paper.

Cook caramels, chocolate pieces and water over low heat, stirring constantly, until caramels and chocolate are melted and mixture is blended. Remove from heat.

Dip each apple into caramel mixture and spread it over apple with a spatula. Press each coated apple into a mound of peanuts, turning to distribute peanuts. Makes 6.

There are more good finger foods in other chapters in this book; consult Index for page numbers.

In Chapter 2, "SNACK BUT STAY SLIM"
        Banana Popsicles
        Blueberry Sicles
        Dilly Cheese-stuffed Celery
        Pineapple Cheese-stuffed Celery
        Raspberry Pops
        Tuna Nibblers

In Chapter 3, "FRUITS AND VEGETABLES"
                 Orange-Ice Cream Pops
                 Orange Pops

In Chapter 7, "SWEETS TO EAT"
                      Applesauce Oatmeal Drops
                      Banana Cookies
                      Cashew-Date Drops
                      Fruited Bran Cookies
                      Good Health Bars
                      Granola Cookies
                      Honeyed Raisin Cookies
                      Molasses Ginger Cookies
                      Oatmeal Fruit Cookies
                      Peanut-Date Balls
                      Pea-nutty Cookies
                      Raisin Carrot Oatmeal Cookies
                      Sunflower Refrigerator Cookies
                      Super Chocolate Chip Cookies

Chapter 2

SNACK BUT STAY SLIM

Snacks can be a big help in supplying the nutrients necessary for good health. But you don't want to eat unneeded calories. If members of your family have difficulty holding down their weight—or losing surplus pounds—you'll want to make it easier for them to snack leanly.

Some of the low-calorie nutritious snacks that taste the best are simple and quick to fix. Serve *skim* milk, for instance. And *fresh* fruits. Fruit juices, too—though you might watch the size of glasses available for pouring juice. It is easy to drink too many calories. (Many canned juices have sugar added; look for "unsweetened" on labels.) And don't forget that water, which has no calories, also quickly quenches thirst. It's a good idea, on a hot day, to offer water first, then juice.

Mothers and the young children at home are the Number One midmorning eaters. This is the ideal time to help a youngster establish habits of eating nutritious foods instead of empty calories. You can also guide him from overeating which researchers say will help make him less prone to overweight in adulthood.

A *small* glass of skim milk, *half* a graham cracker spread with peanut butter, or a *small* peanut butter or meat sandwich and three or four orange sections make a good midmorning meal. Or give the youngster three or four tiny cubes of Cheddar cheese on picks, a petite glass of orange juice and a cracker. Such little meals taste good and rank high in nutrients without being too caloric. And youngsters like to eat finger food.

Specialize in some low-calorie snacks for both yourself and your family—snacks you can fix at your convenience and refrigerate or freeze. If you want to drink less coffee, try our Snacker's Tomato Soup for a midmorning pickup. Choose a saltine, cracker or piece of melba toast for an accompaniment; it will add only fifteen to twenty-five calories. Keep the remainder of the soup in the refrigerator to use the next day or for your husband to enjoy with his bedtime snack.

American men are the great evening snackers. Their dinner hour comes early in comparison with that in most European homes. Sometime before the late newscast, men are often hungry —even though some may be struggling to eat less. Encourage them to team the tomato soup or Mulled Tomato Juice with a Slim Jim Cheeseburger for a low-calorie snack. Some of these home chefs will make their own sandwich while the tomato soup or beverage heats.

Or have Butterscotch Pumpkin Pudding ready in the refrigerator. Most men compliment this dessert which contributes calcium and vitamin A, though some of them cannot refrain from mentioning they wish they were eating pumpkin pie.

Yogurt during the last fifteen years has gained wide acceptance, especially with women, many of whom consider it a diet food. Almost everyone enjoys Blueberry Sicles, made with yogurt and designed primarily for a children's special. One cup of plain yogurt contains the same nutrients and number of calories as the skim and nonfat dry milk from which it is made. Flavored yogurts are sweetened, adding an extra one hundred calories per cup. But before condemning luscious Blueberry Sicles, made with blueberry flavor yogurt, as not qualifying for a low-calorie snack, notice the size of our servings. Since the recipe makes six servings, a single serving is small by any standard.

One mark of a gracious hostess is the type of snacks she shares with informal company. You can count on many guests wishing to avoid sweet, rich and caloric refreshments in an effort to control their weight. They appreciate the hostess's thoughtfulness in offering them low-calorie snacks or at least a choice of foods that include them.

Several hostess recipes in this chapter include Diet Apricot Dessert and Three Fruit and Strawberry Buttermilk Sherbets. Treat a friend to a glass of sparkling Strawberry Fizz. Or set out a bowl of Zesty Cheese Dip with color-bright, crisp raw vegetable dippers. You'll find these and other recipes in this chapter are delicious refreshments but also low-calorie.

MULLED TOMATO JUICE

Good substitute for the midmorning coffee. Serve with whole wheat crackers spread with peanut butter or cheese

1 (46 oz.) can tomato juice	1 tsp. celery salt
2 tblsp. lemon juice	1 tsp. onion salt
1 tblsp. Worcestershire sauce	¼ tsp. dried oregano
	Few drops Tabasco sauce

Combine all ingredients in saucepan. Heat to boiling. Reduce heat and simmer 3 minutes. Or refrigerate without simmering. Heat in amounts as desired. Makes 8 (¾ cup) servings.

STRAWBERRY FIZZ

Serve this drink before the fizz is gone

1 (12 oz.) can pineapple juice, chilled (1½ c.)
1 (10 oz.) pkg. frozen strawberries
2 (16 oz.) bottles low-calorie, lemon-lime carbonated beverage,
    chilled

Combine pineapple juice and strawberries in blender container. Cover and whirl until blended. Pour into large pitcher or bowl. Add carbonated beverage, stir gently and serve at once. Makes 10 servings.

DILLY CHEESE-STUFFED CELERY

Crisp, well seasoned snack that supplies fiber and calcium

1 c. creamed cottage cheese   Celery branches, cut in 3″
1 tblsp. finely chopped green   lengths
    onion   Seasoned salt
⅛ tsp. dried dill weed

Place cheese in blender container. Whirl until smooth. Stir in onion and dill weed. Cover and chill at least ½ hour. Spread in celery branches. Sprinkle with seasoned salt. Makes 1 cup spread.

PINEAPPLE CHEESE-STUFFED CELERY

Another combination of celery and dairy products for nibblers

1 (5 oz.) jar Neufchatel cheese spread with pineapple
3 tblsp. plain yogurt
Celery branches, cut in 3" lengths

Blend together cheese and yogurt. Chill at least ½ hour. Spread in celery branches. Makes ⅔ cup spread.

LOW-CAL CLAM DIP

Cottage cheese is the base for this tasty, low-calorie dip

1 (8 oz.) can minced clams
1½ c. cottage cheese
½ tsp. seasoned salt
2 tsp. lemon juice

1 tsp. Worcestershire sauce
1 tblsp. minced green onion
Assorted crisp vegetable
dippers

In blender container combine clams with liquid, cottage cheese, seasoned salt, lemon juice and Worcestershire sauce. Cover and whirl until smooth. Stir in green onion. Cover and chill at least several hours to blend flavors. Serve with cauliflowerets and strips of carrot, celery, zucchini and/or cucumber. Makes about 2 cups.

FRENCH ONION DIP

Serve with raw vegetable dippers—especially good with celery

1 (8 oz.) carton plain yogurt
1 c. small-curd creamed
cottage cheese

3 tblsp. dry onion soup mix
Few drops Tabasco sauce

Combine all ingredients. Cover and chill at least 3 hours. Makes 2 cups.

ZESTY CHEESE DIP

Serve with raw vegetable dippers, such as celery, carrot and cucumber strips and cauliflowerets

1 (5 oz.) jar Neufchatel
   cheese spread with
   pimiento and olives
1 c. dry cottage cheese
3 tblsp. skim milk

½ tsp. onion salt
¼ tsp. garlic salt
¼ tsp. Worcestershire sauce
Few drops Tabasco sauce

Combine all ingredients in blender container. Whirl until smooth. Chill. Makes about 1 cup.

TUNA NIBBLERS

Colorful, protein-filled and tasty snack. If you must have an accompaniment, choose a crisp cracker or two

1 (6½ oz.) can water-pack
   tuna, drained and flaked
1 (3 oz.) pkg. Neufchatel
   cheese
⅓ c. finely chopped parsley
2 tblsp. finely chopped celery

1 tblsp. finely chopped green
   onion
2 tsp. lemon juice
½ tsp. Worcestershire sauce
¼ tsp. salt

Blend together tuna and cheese. Stir in remaining ingredients. Form heaping teaspoonfuls of mixture in balls. Chill thoroughly. Serve with cocktail picks. Makes 1½ dozen.

SLIMMERS' DEVILED EGGS

High in protein, low in calories—eggs are a snack standby

6 hard-cooked eggs
¼ c. creamed cottage
  cheese
2 tblsp. skim milk
1 tblsp. finely chopped green
  onion and tops

1 tsp. prepared mustard
2 tsp. vinegar
¼ tsp. salt
Dash of pepper
Sprinkling of paprika

Cut eggs in half lengthwise; remove yolks. With fork mash yolks and cottage cheese together until blended; beat in milk. Stir in onion, mustard, vinegar, salt and pepper. Spoon yolk mixture into egg whites. Sprinkle with paprika. Chill. Makes 12.

LOW-CAL BORSCHT

Team vegetable juice with beets for a hot soup. Try a cup of it for a non-caloric midmorning pickup

1 (12 oz.) can vegetable
  juice cocktail
1 (8 oz.) can cubed beets

1 tsp. lemon juice
1 tsp. salt
1 beef bouillon cube

Combine vegetable juice cocktail, beets, lemon juice and salt in blender container. Cover and whirl until smooth. Pour into saucepan. Add bouillon cube and bring to boiling, stirring to dissolve bouillon cube. Serve in cups. Makes 6 servings.

GAZPACHO

Eliminate salad oil if you want to serve a really low-calorie soup.
Especially refreshing between-meal snack in hot weather

3 medium tomatoes, peeled
and finely chopped (2 c.)
½ cucumber, peeled and
finely chopped (½ c.)
¼ c. finely chopped green
pepper
2 tsp. grated onion
1 small garlic clove, minced

½ tsp. salt
⅛ tsp. pepper
2 c. tomato juice
2 tblsp. vegetable or olive
oil
2 tblsp. wine vinegar
Few drops Tabasco sauce

Combine all ingredients. Chill thoroughly. Serve very cold for a summer soup. Makes 6 servings.

BEEF VEGETABLE SOUP

The emphasis in this low-calorie soup is on the vegetables

5 c. water
1 (16 oz.) can tomatoes, cut
up
1½ c. sliced carrots
1 c. chopped onion
¾ c. chopped celery

1 garlic clove, minced
6 beef bouillon cubes
½ tsp. salt
⅛ tsp. pepper
½ lb. ground beef
1 (10 oz.) pkg. frozen peas

In Dutch oven combine water, tomatoes, carrots, onions, celery, garlic, bouillon cubes, salt and pepper. Bring to a boil. Reduce heat and simmer, covered, 10 minutes.

Meanwhile, brown beef in small skillet; pour off excess fat.

Add beef and peas to soup. Bring to a boil. Reduce heat and simmer, covered, 5 minutes.

Remove portion of soup to freeze for snacks. Continue simmering remaining soup, covered, until all the vegetables are tender, about 10 minutes. Makes in all about 2½ quarts.

Soup for Snacks: Ladle ¾ c. soup into 1-cup freezer containers, cool, cover and freeze. To reheat, place container in pan of warm water to loosen soup; turn soup into a small saucepan. Cover and simmer until heated through.

To Use Microwave Oven: Ladle ¾ c. soup into half-pint glass jars or 10 oz. glass casseroles. To reheat, remove metal lids, cover unthawed soup with waxed paper or glass casserole lids and place in microwave oven.

Cook 1 serving on high 3 minutes. Stir; cook 1 minute more.

Cook 2 servings on high 5 minutes. Stir; cook 2½ minutes more.

SNACKER'S TOMATO SOUP

Serve piping hot or chilled in mugs. Soup becomes a little spicier if chilled a day or longer, but not objectionably so

1 (46 oz.) can vegetable juice cocktail	1 tsp. sugar
	¼ tsp. chili powder
1 c. finely chopped celery	⅛ tsp. pepper
2 beef bouillon cubes	

Combine all ingredients in saucepan. Bring to a boil. Reduce heat and simmer, covered, 20 minutes. Serve hot or chilled. Makes 1½ quarts.

YOGURT CUCUMBER SOUP

Try this soup that is famous in many countries. It is very cooling and refreshing in hot weather. Good with tuna sandwiches

2 (8 oz.) cartons plain yogurt
1½ c. water
2 medium cucumbers,
   peeled and thinly sliced
2 tblsp. chopped parsley

1 tblsp. chopped green
   onion
1 tsp. salt
½ tsp. dried dill weed
⅛ tsp. pepper

Blend together yogurt and water. Add remaining ingredients. Cover and chill at least 30 minutes. Soup will keep several days. Makes 5 cups.

DILLED GREEN BEANS

For a color change substitute carrots for the beans. Wash, scrape and cut 2 pounds carrots into slender strips. Cook carrots only 3 minutes and proceed as with the beans

2 lbs. green beans
2 tsp. mustard seed
2 tsp. dried dill weed
1 tsp. dill seed
½ tsp. crushed dried hot
   red pepper

4 garlic cloves
2 c. water
2 c. white vinegar
⅔ c. sugar
2 tblsp. salt

Snip ends from beans and wash thoroughly. Cook in boiling, salted water 5 minutes; drain.

Meanwhile, in each of 2 (1 qt.) glass jars place 1 tsp. mustard seed, 1 tsp. dill weed, ½ tsp. dill seed, ¼ tsp. crushed red pepper and 2 garlic cloves. Pack beans in jars.

In saucepan combine water, vinegar, sugar and salt. Bring to a boil. Pour over green beans. Cool, cover and refrigerate overnight. Will keep in refrigerator up to 2 weeks. Makes 2 quarts.

VEGETABLE SLAW

Salad is on the tart side. A little sugar would improve the flavor for many people without adding too many calories

6 c. shredded
   cabbage (½ medium
   head)
1 c. grated carrots
1 (8 oz.) can French-style
   green beans, drained
½ c. chopped green pepper

¼ c. chopped onion
½ c. vinegar
3 tblsp. vegetable oil
2 tblsp. chopped parsley
1 tsp. dry mustard
¾ tsp. salt
⅛ tsp. pepper

Combine vegetables in bowl. Stir together remaining ingredients. Pour over vegetables; toss. Serve immediately or cover and chill up to 3 days. Makes 2 quarts.

CABBAGE VEGETABLE SLAW

Pretty orange and green salad contributes vitamins C and A

1 qt. grated cabbage
1 c. grated carrot
½ c. finely chopped green
   pepper

¼ c. sugar
2 tsp. salt
½ c. cider vinegar
½ c. water

In large bowl combine cabbage, carrot and green pepper. Sprinkle with sugar and salt. Add vinegar and water, mixing thoroughly. Cover and refrigerate. Let stand at least one hour before using. Salad will keep 1 week. Makes about twelve servings.

MEDITERRANEAN SALAD

Yogurt and lemon juice makes a dressing the consistency of Italian dressing for this vegetable refrigerator salad

2 small zucchini, thinly sliced	¼ c. chopped green onion
1 cucumber, peeled and thinly sliced	¼ c. chopped parsley
	1½ tsp. salt
1 tomato, chopped	½ c. plain yogurt
1 c. shredded cabbage	1 tblsp. lemon juice
	¼ tsp. dried dill weed

Combine vegetables in bowl. Stir in salt. Cover and refrigerate 1 hour; drain. Combine remaining ingredients. Stir into vegetables. Cover and chill at least 2 hours or up to 24 hours. Makes 8 servings.

BROCCOLI SALAD

An unusual refrigerator vegetable salad containing the valuable nutrients of broccoli, buttermilk and eggs

2 (10 oz.) pkgs. frozen broccoli spears	¼ c. chopped dill pickle
½ c. buttermilk	½ tsp. salt
⅓ c. low-calorie, mayonnaise-type salad dressing	¼ tsp. parsley flakes
	⅛ tsp. pepper
	⅛ tsp. garlic powder
2 hard-cooked eggs, chopped	⅛ tsp. onion powder

Place broccoli in 1 c. boiling salted water. Cover and cook until broccoli can be separated. Separate spears and continue cooking until tender-crisp, about 4 minutes. Drain. Blend together buttermilk and salad dressing. Stir in remaining ingredients. Pour over broccoli. Toss gently. Cover and refrigerate several hours. Makes 6 servings.

SLIM JIM CHEESEBURGER

You cook the meat on the bread. Sandwich is filling but has only 230 calories. Easy to make with toaster-broiler oven

1 slice rye bread	1 tsp. ketchup
⅛ lb. ground round beef	1 thin onion slice
(about ¼ c.)	1 slice mozzarella cheese
Salt and pepper	(¾ oz.)

Toast bread on one side. Cover untoasted side with ground beef, spreading to edges. Broil 2 to 4″ from heat until browned, 5 to 6 minutes. Sprinkle with salt and pepper. Spread with ketchup. Top with onion slice, then cheese slice. Return to broiler just until cheese melts, 1 to 2 minutes. Makes 1 serving.

EGG SALAD SANDWICHES

Serve these open-face sandwiches to the breakfast skippers for a midmorning snack. Good with tomato juice

3 hard-cooked eggs,	2 tblsp. chopped dill pickle
chopped	2 tsp. chopped onion
2 tblsp. low-calorie	1 tsp. prepared mustard
mayonnaise-type salad	⅛ tsp. salt
dressing	4 slices whole wheat bread,
¼ c. chopped celery	toasted

Combine eggs, salad dressing, celery, pickle, onion, mustard and salt. Spread on hot toast. Makes about 1 cup, enough for 4 sandwiches.

TUNA SALAD SANDWICHES

Make the salad in the morning, cover and chill. Let youngsters make their own sandwiches when they return from school

1 (6½ oz.) can water-pack
　tuna, drained
⅓ c. creamed cottage
　cheese
⅓ c. chopped celery
3 tblsp. chopped dill pickle
1 tblsp. chopped onion

2 tblsp. low-calorie
　mayonnaise-type salad
　dressing
2 tsp. lemon juice
5 slices bread or toast
5 slices tomato (optional)

Combine tuna, cottage cheese, celery, pickle, onion, salad dressing and lemon juice. Cover and refrigerate at least ½ hour. Spread on bread or toast and top each sandwich with tomato slice. Makes 1½ cups salad mixture, enough for 5 open-face sandwiches.

BLUEBERRY SICLES

Anyone who likes blueberries will score this treat 100 per cent

**2 c. fresh blueberries or 1 (9 oz.) carton frozen blueberries
1 (8 oz.) carton blueberry flavor yogurt**

Combine blueberries and yogurt in blender. Cover and whirl until smooth. Pour into 6 (3½ oz.) paper drinking cups. Partially freeze; insert wooden sticks. Freeze firm. To eat, tear off paper cup. Makes 6.

PEACHY CHEESE DESSERT

Serve this over sliced fresh peaches when they are in season

1 c. large-curd creamed cottage cheese
1 (8 oz.) carton peach flavor yogurt

Combine cottage cheese and yogurt. Cover and chill at least 30 minutes. Makes 2 cups or 4 servings.

STRAWBERRY BUTTERMILK SHERBET

Buttermilk adds nutritive value to this appetizing sherbet

2 (10 oz.) pkgs. frozen strawberries, thawed
1 envelope unflavored gelatin
1½ c. buttermilk

Drain strawberries, reserving syrup. Place ½ c. syrup in small saucepan. Sprinkle gelatin over syrup. Heat until gelatin is dissolved, stirring constantly. Combine with remaining syrup, strawberries and buttermilk in metal bowl.

Cover and freeze until mixture is partially frozen, 2 to 4 hours. Stir occasionally. With chilled beater, beat at medium speed until smooth, scraping bowl constantly. Spread in 8½ ×4½ ×2½" loaf pan. Cover and freeze firm. Makes 6 servings.

THREE FRUIT SHERBET

Delightful blending of fruit flavors earns praise for this dessert. The natural sugar in fruit is the only sweetening

4 large bananas
2 c. orange juice
1 (8 oz.) can unsweetened crushed pineapple

Mash bananas until smooth. Stir in remaining ingredients. Pour into a 9″ square pan. Cover with foil or plastic wrap. Freeze until partially frozen.

Turn out into chilled mixer bowl and beat with chilled beater at medium speed until smooth, but still frozen. Return mixture to pan; cover. Freeze firm. Makes about 12 servings.

RASPBERRY POPS

Sweeter than some low-calorie desserts but servings are small

1 (3 oz.) pkg. raspberry flavor gelatin
1 c. boiling water
1 (8 oz.) carton raspberry flavor yogurt

Dissolve gelatin in boiling water. Chill until partially set. Add yogurt and beat with electric mixer until thoroughly combined. Pour into 6 (3½ oz.) paper drinking cups. Place in freezer. When partially frozen, insert wooden stick in each. Freeze firm. Store in freezer in plastic bag. To eat, peel off paper. Makes 6.

BANANA POPSICLES

This is a small snack you can serve to an overweight child

1 c. orange juice
3 bananas, cut in chunks
2 tblsp. sugar
1 tblsp. lemon juice

Combine ingredients in blender container. Cover and whirl just until blended. Pour into 7 (3½ oz.) paper drinking cups. Place in freezer. When partially frozen, insert wooden stick in each. Freeze firm. Store in freezer in plastic bag. To eat, peel off paper cup. Makes 7.

WINTERTIME MINTED FRUIT CUP

Add a few frozen, unsweetened blueberries or strawberries if you like. Fruit cup will keep up to 8 hours in refrigerator

2 oranges
1 (20 oz.) can unsweetened
 pineapple chunks
1 banana, peeled and sliced

1 unpeeled apple, cored and
 chopped
1 tblsp. honey
1 tsp. dried mint

Peel and section oranges over a bowl, reserving juice. Combine with remaining ingredients. Cover and refrigerate at least ½ hour. Will keep up to 8 hours. Makes 1 quart or 8 servings.

DIET APRICOT DESSERT

This low-calorie frozen dessert in no way sacrifices flavor

1 (16 oz.) can diet-pack apricot halves, drained
⅛ tsp. ground cinnamon
1 qt. vanilla ice milk, softened

In large bowl mash apricots with fork. Stir in cinnamon. Add ice milk. Quickly swirl apricots with a fork. Return to ice milk container, cover and freeze. Makes 8 to 10 servings.

PEACHES WITH SPICY YOGURT

Honey and cinnamon contribute interesting flavor to the fruit

1 (16 oz.) can sliced
 diet-pack peaches, chilled
 and drained

½ c. plain yogurt
1 tblsp. honey
⅛ tsp. ground cinnamon

Place peaches in 4 (6 oz.) custard cups. Combine remaining ingredients. Spoon over peaches. Makes 4 servings.

CRANBERRY ORANGE SHERBET

The fruit juices add to the day's vitamin C intake

½ c. sugar
1½ tsp. unflavored gelatin
  (½ envelope)
Dash of salt

1½ c. low-calorie cranberry
  juice cocktail
½ c. orange juice

Combine sugar, gelatin and salt in saucepan. Stir in 1 c. cranberry juice cocktail. Heat and stir over medium heat until sugar and gelatin are dissolved. Remove from heat. Stir in remaining ½ c. cranberry juice cocktail and orange juice.

Pour into 9×5×3" loaf pan. Cover and freeze until firm. Break in chunks and place in chilled bowl of electric mixer. Beat until smooth. Return to loaf pan, cover and freeze firm. Makes 6 servings.

BUTTERSCOTCH PUMPKIN PUDDING

Pumpkin and skim milk are the nutrition rewards in this dessert

1 (3⅝ oz.) pkg. regular
  butterscotch pudding and
  pie filling
2 c. skim milk
1 (16 oz.) can pumpkin

2 tsp. sugar
½ tsp. ground cinnamon
¼ tsp. ground ginger
¼ tsp. salt
⅛ tsp. ground cloves

Prepare pudding as directed on package, using skim milk. Stir in remaining ingredients. Spoon into 8 (6 oz.) custard cups or a bowl. Cover and chill. Makes 8 servings.

There are more good low-calorie snacks in other recipes in this book; consult Index for page numbers.

In Chapter 3, "FRUITS AND VEGETABLES"
> Carrot Slaw
> Confetti Sauerkraut Salad
> Fruit-Yogurt Combo
> Garden Tomato Juice
> Marinated Tomatoes
> Mixed Vegetable Relish
> Orange Cider Punch
> Orange Pops
> Refrigerator Carrot Salad
> Salsa

In Chapter 5, "MILK . . . STILL THE DEPENDABLE"
> Dilled Cheese Dip
> Strawberry Dip
> Zippy Beef Dip

Chapter 3

CAPITALIZE ON FRUITS AND VEGETABLES

You can step up your family's health by keeping your refrigerator stocked with more fruits and vegetables for snacking. They provide vitamins, iron and other minerals, all of which are frequently in short supply in American meals. They also contribute needed fiber. Carrot and celery sticks and apples are long-established favorites, but other orchard and garden produce can become popular, too.

To win approval for these snacks may take some planning and imagination. But if you expose your husband and children to foods you want them to eat by making them easily and quickly available, you're on the way.

In your effort to add vitamins to the day's fare, don't overlook beverages. Take, for example, fruit juice pickups such as Tropical Fruit Shake, Pink Frost and Orange Cider Punch made by recipes in this chapter. Prepare them and chill in a pitcher. That invites the snacker to reach for a glass and pour his own drink, instead of opening a soft drink bottle.

Freeze fruit juices on sticks for pops to hand to small children on hot days. Our Orange Pops and Orange-Ice Cream Pops, for instance, will really please them.

Get acquainted with a variety of refrigerator salads—an excellent way to put some of the important dark green and deep yellow vegetables on your family's favored snack list. The collection of recipes in this chapter will delight you. They are a cross between salads and relishes, and you can store them, covered, in the refrigerator for a few days. They can be spooned out quickly and are a great accompaniment to sandwiches.

The first taste of Refrigerator Carrot Salad surprises everyone. And men who like blue cheese praise Blue Cheese Onions and Blue Cheese Tomatoes. Tuck them in hamburgers or other meat sandwiches, or serve as a side dish snack.

Try our Italian Chef's Salad Mix. Combine slender strips of cheese, cooked ham, chicken or roast beef, pepperoni and green pepper with drained kidney beans and onion. Put in a plastic bag and chill in the refrigerator alongside a bag of cleaned, crisp greens and a bottle of salad dressing. Anyone can toss his own chef's salad in a minute.

Orange juice is a common source of vitamin C. It can be the frozen type, or squeezed from the fresh fruit. They both contain about the same amounts of nutrients. Among the leading vitamin C foods are oranges, grapefruit, limes and lemons and their juices, fresh raw strawberries, tomatoes and tomato juice, cantaloupe and such vegetables as green and red peppers, leafy greens (the darker green the better), broccoli and cabbage. The degree of freshness is the best indicator of the vitamin C content in garden produce; as the produce loses its freshness, the vitamin C content is reduced. The acid in citrus fruits and tomatoes serves to protect their vitamin C. That means you can store orange juice or tomato juice in the refrigerator, covered, in glass, plastic or waxed containers without losing vitamin C.

All dark green and deep yellow vegetables and yellow fruits like cantaloupe, dried apricots and peaches, are good contributors of vitamin A. They contain carotene which, during metabolism, is turned into vitamin A.

Eating fruits and vegetables between meals improves the daily diet for almost all families. These foods make good snacks because they contribute important nutrients and are not likely to destroy appetites for dinner. The recipes in this chapter will help you make selections that promote good health and taste extra-good.

FRUIT DRINKS AND FROZEN POP-SNACKS

TROPICAL FRUIT SHAKE

Most little children like this easy to make, energy-charged drink

   1 c. orange juice
   1 banana, cut in chunks
   1 c. vanilla ice cream

Combine ingredients in blender container. Cover and whirl just until smooth. Makes about 2 cups.

PINK FROST

Perfect snack to serve with Christmas cookies. The bottled cranberry juice cocktail is fortified with vitamin C

   1 c. chilled cranberry juice cocktail
   ½ c. chilled orange juice
   1 pt. vanilla ice cream

Combine all ingredients in blender container. Cover and whirl just until blended. Makes about 3 cups.

APPLE CRANBERRY PITCHER PUNCH

Pink of perfection in taste and color. A source of vitamin C

1 (32 oz.) bottle cranberry-apple drink
1 (6 oz.) can frozen lemonade concentrate
1 (28 oz.) bottle carbonated water

Combine cranberry-apple drink and lemonade concentrate. Cover and store in the refrigerator. To serve pour cranberry mixture over ice in glass, two thirds full. Add carbonated water and stir gently. Makes about 5 cups cranberry mixture, or 7 servings.

PITCHER GRAPE PUNCH

Chill grape juice-lemonade mixture in a pitcher ready to pour

1 (24 oz.) bottle grape juice
1 (6 oz.) can frozen lemonade concentrate
1 (28 oz.) bottle carbonated water

Combine grape juice and lemonade concentrate in a pitcher. Cover and store in refrigerator. To serve, pour grape mixture over ice in glass, two thirds full. Add carbonated water and stir gently. Makes 3½ cups grape mixture, or 6 servings.

GOLDEN GRAPE PUNCH

Everyone who sips this golden punch is surprised by its luscious grape flavor. Serve it on special occasions

1 (6 oz.) can frozen orange juice concentrate
1½ c. bottled white grape juice
¼ c. lemon juice
¼ c. honey
1 (16 oz.) bottle lemon-lime carbonated beverage

Reconstitute orange juice concentrate as directed on can. Stir in grape juice, lemon juice and honey. Carefully add carbonated beverage. Serve in ice-filled glasses. Makes 7 cups or 10 servings.

FRIENDSHIP PUNCH

Half the enjoyment of this hot punch is the spicy fragrance that permeates the house. Serve to friends on a cold afternoon with Pea-nutty and Refrigerator Sunflower Cookies

1 (32 oz.) bottle cranberry
   juice cocktail
2 (6 oz.) cans pineapple
   juice (1½ c.)
⅔ c. water
Dash of salt
⅓ c. brown sugar, firmly
   packed

2 tsp. whole cloves
1 (6″) stick cinnamon,
   broken in pieces
Peel of ¼ orange, cut in
   strips

In 9-cup automatic percolator combine cranberry juice cocktail, pineapple juice, water, salt and brown sugar. Place whole cloves, cinnamon stick and orange peel in basket. (Remove most of bitter white portion from orange peel.)

Assemble coffee maker, plug in and perk. Makes 9 servings.

ORANGE CIDER PUNCH

Switcheroo for Halloween! The citrus fruit juices add vitamin C to cider; cider gives orange juice a new taste

1 qt. apple cider
2 c. orange juice

½ c. lemon juice
¼ c. sugar

Combine all ingredients. Chill in refrigerator or serve over ice. Makes about 6½ cups.

FROSTY ORANGE NOG

Excellent midmorning pickup for the child who refuses breakfast. The orange juice supplies the daily requirements of vitamin C and the ice cream as much calcium as ½ cup milk. The egg contributes a variety of other nutrients

½ c. orange juice
1 egg
1 c. vanilla ice cream

Combine ingredients in blender container. Cover and whirl just until smooth. Makes about 1⅓ cups.

NOTE: Use only clean, whole (not cracked) eggs in eggnog or any recipe calling for eggs which will not be cooked.

ORANGE POPS

Freeze orange juice on sticks for a hot weather treat for little children. Or try grape, pineapple or apple juice frozen concentrate; pops will have less vitamin C, but a change of flavor often sharpens appetites

1 (6 oz.) can frozen orange juice concentrate
1 juice can water

Combine orange juice and water. Pour into 5 (3½ oz.) paper cups. Freeze until mushy. Insert wooden or plastic sticks. Freeze until firm. Store in freezer in plastic bag. To eat, peel off paper cup. Makes 5 servings.

ORANGE-ICE CREAM POPS

You need not be a nutrition expert to recognize that milk, orange juice and ice cream add up to worthy pop-snacks for children. And they taste so good

1 c. milk
1 (6 oz.) can orange juice concentrate, partly thawed
1 pt. vanilla ice cream

Combine all ingredients in blender container; cover and blend until smooth. Pour into 8 (3½ oz.) paper cups. Place in freezer. When partially frozen, insert wooden stick in each. Freeze firm. Store in freezer in plastic bag. To eat, peel off paper cup. Makes 8 servings.

APPETIZERS AND SOUPS

GARDEN TOMATO JUICE

Splendid way to use a bountiful tomato crop. Men especially like the Tomato Juice Piquant variation. For a hearty, nutritious snack, serve with a grilled cheese sandwich

12 medium tomatoes, peeled, cored and chopped (about 4 lbs.)	½ bay leaf
	½ c. water
	1½ tsp. salt
1 (8″) celery branch	½ tsp. sugar
4 sprigs parsley	¼ tsp. paprika
1 slice onion	

Combine tomatoes, celery, parsley, onion, bay leaf and water in Dutch oven. Bring to a boil. Reduce heat and simmer, covered, 20 minutes. Press through sieve. Add salt, sugar and paprika. Chill thoroughly. Makes about 5½ cups.

Tomato Juice Piquant: Combine 1 qt. Garden Tomato Juice with 4 tsp. lemon juice, 2 tsp. Worcestershire sauce and a few drops Tabasco sauce.

POOR MAN'S CAVIAR

People not fond of eggplant enjoy it in this Mideastern dip

1 large eggplant (1½ lbs.)	1 c. chopped onion
1 clove garlic, minced	2 tsp. salt
⅓ c. vegetable or olive oil	⅛ tsp. pepper
2 large tomatoes, peeled and chopped	2 tblsp. lemon juice
	2 tblsp. chopped parsley

Bake eggplant in 400° oven until soft, 30 to 35 minutes. Peel and chop.

In skillet cook garlic in oil over low heat 2 minutes. Add eggplant, tomatoes, onion, salt and pepper. Cover and cook over low heat 20 minutes, stirring occasionally. Uncover and continue cooking, stirring frequently, 20 minutes or until mixture is thick.

Mash with potato masher. Stir in lemon juice. Place in bowl, cover and chill. Sprinkle with parsley and serve with crackers or rye bread. Makes about 3 cups.

READY-TO-POUR BEAN SOUP

Soup stays hot on the counter top in a vacuum bottle, ready for the younger children to serve themselves when they return from school. Mother knows it pleases them to fill their own mugs or bowls. To boost the quality of the protein when your family snacks on this bean soup, offer a cheese spread on crackers or whole wheat bread

1 (18 oz.) jar baked beans	1 tsp. instant minced onion
1 (14 oz.) can beef broth	½ tsp. salt
1 (8 oz.) can stewed tomatoes	⅛ tsp. pepper

Combine beans, broth and tomatoes in blender container. Cover and blend just until smooth. Pour into large saucepan. Add onion, salt and pepper. Bring to a boil. Reduce heat and simmer, uncovered, 15 minutes. Pour into vacuum bottle. Shake before serving. Makes 1 quart.

CHILLED BORSCHT

Most appetizing on a hot summer day served with sandwiches.

8 medium beets, peeled and shredded (5 c.)	2 medium potatoes, peeled and cut in ½" cubes (1½ c.)
1½ c. chopped onion	⅓ c. lemon juice
10 c. water	1½ tblsp. sugar
10 chicken bouillon cubes	Dairy sour cream
1 tblsp. salt	

Combine beets, onion, water, bouillon cubes and salt in Dutch oven. Bring to a boil. Reduce heat and simmer, covered, 15 minutes. Add potatoes. Continue simmering 15 minutes. Remove from heat and stir in lemon juice and sugar. Cool, cover and chill in refrigerator.

Serve chilled soup in bowls and garnish each serving with a dollop of sour cream. Soup will keep in refrigerator up to a week. Makes about 3½ quarts.

REFRIGERATOR SALADS

BLUE CHEESE ONIONS

Peppy way to fix onions for hamburgers, meat sandwiches, and steak—men's favorite. Tightly covered, mixture will keep several days in refrigerator

½ c. crumbled blue cheese (2 oz.)	⅛ tsp. pepper
	⅛ tsp. paprika
¼ c. vegetable oil	2 large onions, thinly sliced
2 tblsp. lemon juice	and separated into rings
¼ tsp. salt	

In bowl mash blue cheese with oil, lemon juice, salt, pepper and paprika until blended. Add onion rings and toss. Cover and chill several hours or overnight, stirring occasionally.

Serve with broiled ground beef patties in buns, or cold beef sandwiches. Makes enough for 12 sandwiches.

BLUE CHEESE TOMATOES

Serve to family at noon; save leftovers for after-school snacks

3 tomatoes, peeled and
   thinly sliced
3 tblsp. vegetable oil
2 tblsp. wine or cider
   vinegar

½ c. crumbled blue cheese
   (2 oz.)
¼ tsp. salt
⅛ tsp. pepper

Place tomatoes in bowl. Stir together remaining ingredients. Pour over tomatoes and toss gently. Cover and refrigerate several hours or overnight.

Serve on hamburgers or cold meat sandwiches, or with lettuce for a quick salad. Makes about 6 salads or enough for 12 sandwiches.

MARINATED TOMATOES

Tempting make-ahead salad is a garden-season special

6 tomatoes, peeled
½ c. vegetable oil
¼ c. wine vinegar
¼ c. chopped parsley
¼ c. chopped green onion

1 small clove garlic, minced
1 tsp. salt
½ tsp. dried marjoram
   leaves, crushed
¼ tsp. pepper

Place tomatoes in a deep bowl. Vigorously stir together remaining ingredients. Pour over tomatoes. Cover and chill several hours, or overnight. Spoon dressing over tomatoes occasionally. Makes 6 servings.

VEGETABLE MARINADE

Smart way to add vegetables to burgers, cold roast beef and ham sandwiches. Or serve as a side dish instead of having salad

3 tomatoes, peeled and
   thinly sliced
1 medium red onion, sliced
   and separated into rings
¼ c. lemon juice

¼ c. vegetable oil
1 tblsp. chopped parsley
½ tsp. salt
¼ tsp. pepper

Combine tomatoes and onions. Stir together lemon juice, oil, parsley, salt and pepper. Pour over vegetables and toss gently. Refrigerate, covered, for several hours. Drain before serving. Makes about 6 servings of relish or enough for 8 to 10 sandwiches.

SALSA

The flavor of chilies strengthens somewhat during chilling, but not enough to displease people who like Mexican food

4 medium tomatoes, peeled
   and finely chopped
½ c. finely chopped onion
½ c. finely chopped celery
¼ c. finely chopped green
   pepper

2 tblsp. finely chopped
   canned green chilies
2 tblsp. wine vinegar
1 tsp. salt
¼ tsp. dried basil, crushed
⅛ tsp. pepper

Combine all ingredients. Cover and chill several hours or overnight, stirring occasionally. Serve as a dip with corn or tortilla chips or as a relish on hamburgers, tacos or meat sandwiches. Makes about 3½ cups.

REFRIGERATOR CARROT SALAD

One of the best refrigerator salads ever invented. Carrots supply carotene which the body converts to vitamin A; cooking softens the carrots, making the carotene more available. This salad with carrots and green pepper is rich in vitamin A

**2 lbs. carrots, sliced
crosswise
1 (10 oz.) can condensed
tomato soup
½ c. sugar
½ c. vegetable oil
½ c. vinegar**

**1 tsp. salt
¼ tsp. pepper
1 onion, peeled, sliced and
separated into rings
1 green pepper, sliced in
strips**

In large saucepan cover carrots with boiling salted water. Bring to a boil and cook, covered, until tender-crisp, about 7 minutes. Drain.

Blend together soup, sugar, oil, vinegar, salt and pepper; stir into carrots along with onion and green pepper. Cover and refrigerate at least 4 hours. It will keep in refrigerator up to 5 days. Makes 2 quarts.

SUCCOTASH SALAD

Gorgeous color, marvelous taste; yellow corn and bright pimientos contribute vitamin A. Make your own salad dressing if you like, but go easy on garlic. Its flavor strengthens during chilling. Salad may be kept up to eight days.

**1 (10 oz.) pkg. frozen cut
green beans
1 (10 oz.) pkg. frozen corn
1 (4 oz.) jar sliced
pimientos, drained and
chopped**

**¾ c. chopped celery
2 tblsp. finely chopped onion
½ c. bottled French
dressing with garlic**

Cook beans and corn in boiling salted water following package directions. Drain thoroughly. Combine with remaining ingredients. Cover and chill 4 hours or overnight, stirring occasionally. Makes 4 cups or 8 servings.

CARROT SLAW

Spread this on peanut butter sandwiches made with whole wheat bread for something special in taste and good nutrition. Sandwich contributes protein, vitamin A, some of the B-vitamins and iron to the daily diet.

2 c. shredded carrots
½ c. thinly sliced celery
½ c. raisins

½ c. mayonnaise or salad dressing

Combine carrots, celery, raisins and mayonnaise. If not ready to use, cover and store in the refrigerator. Makes about 2 cups or enough for 6 sandwiches.

ITALIAN POTATO SALAD

The combination of celery, onion and pimientos accounts for the superior flavor of this color-bright salad. Cook potatoes in their skins to conserve vitamin C and minerals. Great snack with leftover fried chicken or cheese sandwich

2 (9 oz.) pkgs. frozen Italian green beans
4 c. cooked, peeled, diced potatoes (4 to 5 medium)
½ c. chopped celery
2 tblsp. chopped green onion
1 (2 oz.) jar pimientos, drained and chopped

⅓ c. vinegar
⅓ c. salad oil
1 tsp. salt
⅛ tsp. pepper
⅓ c. dairy sour cream
⅓ c. mayonnaise or salad dressing

Cook beans in boiling salted water following package directions, only until beans are tender-crisp. Drain.

Combine beans, potatoes, celery, onion and pimiento in bowl. Add vinegar, oil, salt and pepper. Cool and chill.

Combine sour cream and mayonnaise. Gently stir into vegetables. Cover and chill several hours or overnight. Stir occasionally. Makes 2 quarts.

ITALIAN CHEF'S SALAD MIX

Use this recipe as a guide and make your own salad mix using foods on hand. Try chicken, turkey, cold roast beef, other cheeses and different salad dressings

1 (6 oz.) pkg. sliced Swiss
  cheese, cut in strips
4 oz. boiled ham, cut in
  strips
2 oz. pepperoni, cut in strips
1 (8 oz.) can kidney beans,
  drained and rinsed

1 green pepper, cut in strips
2 tblsp. chopped onion
Lettuce
Bottled Italian salad
  dressing

Toss together cheese, ham, pepperoni, kidney beans, green pepper and onion. Store in tightly closed plastic bag in refrigerator.

To serve, shred lettuce into individual bowls. Add salad mix topping. (Use 1 c. torn lettuce with ½ c. mix.) Toss with salad dressing. Makes about 1 quart salad mix or 8 servings.

PARMESAN GARDEN SALAD BOWL

Attractive and nutritious way to serve your garden's gifts

3 small zucchini, sliced
1 small head cauliflower,
  broken in small buds
2 tomatoes, cut in wedges
½ c. vegetable oil
⅓ c. vinegar
¼ c. grated Parmesan
  cheese

2 tblsp. chopped parsley
1½ tsp. garlic salt
¼ tsp. pepper
¼ tsp. dried oregano leaves,
  crushed

Combine zucchini, cauliflower and tomatoes in large salad bowl. Combine remaining ingredients in jar with screw-top lid. Shake vigorously. Pour over vegetables; toss gently. Cover and refrigerate several hours or overnight. Makes 8 servings.

CONFETTI SAUERKRAUT SALAD

Carrots, green pepper and pimiento glorify this salad with color and an abundance of vitamin A. Good accompaniment for hearty sandwiches and other main-dish snacks

1 (16 oz.) can sauerkraut
1 c. shredded carrot
1 c. chopped green pepper
1 c. chopped celery

½ c. sugar
½ c. chopped onion
1 (2 oz.) jar pimiento,
  drained and chopped

Combine undrained sauerkraut with remaining ingredients. Cover and refrigerate at least 2 hours before using. Stir occasionally. Salad will keep up to a week in the refrigerator. Makes about 5 cups.

BAKED BEAN SALAD

Beans are a source of good protein but lack some of the essential amino acids in complete proteins. Snack planners can overcome this by adding cheese to the beans

1 (31 oz.) can pork and beans with tomato sauce
1 c. thinly sliced celery
½ c. sliced green onion
½ c. chopped carrot
½ c. sweet pickle relish
½ c. cubed sharp Cheddar cheese

1 large tomato, peeled and diced
½ c. vinegar
¼ c. vegetable oil
1 tsp. salt
⅛ tsp. pepper
1 tsp. prepared mustard

Drain beans, reserving liquid. Discard pork fat. Combine beans with celery, onion, carrot, pickle relish, cheese and tomato.

Combine remaining ingredients. Stir in 2 tblsp. reserved bean liquid. Mix gently into vegetable mixture. Cover and refrigerate 4 hours, or overnight, stirring occasionally. It will keep in refrigerator at least 3 days. Makes 6 cups.

MEXICAN BEAN SALAD

Chili powder and green pepper accent this Southwestern salad

3 tblsp. vegetable oil
3 tblsp. vinegar
1 small clove garlic, minced
½ tsp. salt
½ tsp. chili powder
1 (15 oz.) can pinto beans, drained and rinsed

1 (15 oz.) can kidney beans, drained and rinsed
¾ c. chopped celery
1 medium onion, sliced and separated into rings
¼ c. chopped green pepper

Combine oil, vinegar, garlic, salt and chili powder in mixing bowl. Add remaining ingredients. Toss gently. Cover and refrigerate several hours or overnight. Stir occasionally. It will keep 3 days in refrigerator. Makes 5 cups.

MARINATED VEGETABLES

Broccoli gradually is working its way into salad bowls. Try it in this tasty medley of marinated vegetables. It contributes vivid green color, flavor and nutrients like vitamin A and calcium

2 carrots, cut in sticks
1 c. broccoli buds
1 c. cauliflowerets
1 medium cucumber, peeled and cut in sticks
1 small zucchini, cut in sticks
1 small onion, sliced and separated in rings

1 tomato, cut in wedges
½ c. vegetable oil
3 tblsp. wine vinegar
1 tsp. dried oregano, crushed
1 tsp. salt
¼ tsp. pepper
1 small clove garlic, minced

In saucepan cook carrots, covered, in boiling water 2 minutes. Add broccoli and cauliflower and continue cooking 2 minutes. Drain. Combine with remaining vegetables.

Beat together oil, vinegar, oregano, salt, pepper and garlic. Pour over vegetables and toss gently. Cover and refrigerate at least 8 hours, stirring occasionally. Mixture will keep in refrigerator several days. Makes about 5½ cups.

MIXED VEGETABLE SALAD

Easy cold weather salad made with canned foods as a base

1 (12 oz.) can corn with
  green peppers and
  pimiento, drained
1 (8 oz.) can cut green
  beans, drained
1 (8 oz.) can peas, drained
1 (8 oz.) can kidney beans,
  drained and rinsed
1 c. chopped celery

2 tblsp. chopped onion
2 hard-cooked eggs,
  chopped
¼ c. dairy sour cream
¼ c. mayonnaise or salad
  dressing
1 tsp. prepared mustard
1 tsp. Worcestershire sauce
½ tsp. salt

Combine vegetables and eggs. Blend together remaining ingredients. Add to vegetable mixture; toss gently. Cover and chill at least 4 hours. Makes 5½ cups, or 10 servings.

ORANGE AND YELLOW SALAD

Colorful vegetable relish salad to have ready in the refrigerator

1 c. sliced carrots
⅓ c. sugar
⅓ c. vinegar
2 tblsp. vegetable oil
½ tsp. celery seeds
¼ tsp. salt

⅛ tsp. pepper
1 (17 oz.) can whole kernel
  corn, drained
½ c. chopped green pepper
¼ c. chopped onion

Cook carrots in boiling, salted water until tender-crisp, about 5 minutes. Drain.

In bowl combine sugar, vinegar, oil, celery seeds, salt and pepper. Add carrots, corn, green pepper and onion. Toss gently. Cover and refrigerate at least 4 hours or overnight. Stir occasionally. Makes 3½ cups, or 6 servings.

MIXED VEGETABLE RELISH

Tart vegetable accompaniment to sandwiches—keep it on hand

3 large tomatoes, peeled
1 green pepper
2 branches celery
1 medium zucchini
1 medium onion
½ large cucumber
¾ c. vinegar

¼ c. vegetable oil
¼ c. chopped parsley
1 tsp. sugar
1 tsp. salt
1 tsp. garlic salt
½ tsp. pepper

Coarsely chop vegetables. Stir together vinegar, oil, parsley, sugar, salt, garlic salt and pepper. Stir into vegetables. Cover and chill 4 hours or overnight, stirring occasionally. To serve, remove vegetables with slotted spoon. Makes about 7 cups.

DILLED PINEAPPLE-CUCUMBER SALAD

A refreshing fruit and vegetable salad to make ahead. Nutritionists advise peeling cucumbers—and other vegetables and fruits that are waxed—before eating them

1 (20 oz.) can pineapple
  chunks, drained
1 medium cucumber, peeled
  and sliced
¼ c. dairy sour cream

1 tblsp. mayonnaise or salad
  dressing
½ tsp. salt
⅛ tsp. dried dill weed

Combine all ingredients. Chill at least one hour. Salad keeps well for several hours. Makes 6 servings.

FRUIT-YOGURT COMBO

Rich in vitamin C—serve as a salad or for dessert

1 (20 oz.) can unsweetened
   pineapple chunks
4 tsp. cornstarch
1 tblsp. sugar
½ tsp. grated orange peel

½ c. plain yogurt
3 medium oranges
1 c. seedless green grapes or
   seeded table grapes

Drain pineapple, reserving juice. In saucepan combine cornstarch and sugar. Blend in juice. Cook, stirring constantly, until mixture comes to a boil. Boil 1 minute. Remove from heat; let cool 10 minutes. Stir in orange peel and yogurt.

Peel, section and coarsely cut up oranges, catching the juice. Add pineapple, oranges with juice and grapes to yogurt mixture. Mix lightly. Cover and refrigerate. Makes 1 quart or 8 servings.

Fruits and vegetables are important ingredients in other recipes in this book; consult Index for page numbers.

In Chapter 2, "SNACK BUT STAY SLIM"
            Beef Vegetable Soup
            Broccoli Salad
            Cabbage Vegetable Slaw
            Dilled Green Beans
            Dilly Cheese-stuffed Celery
            Gazpacho
            Low-Cal Borscht
            Mediterranean Salad
            Mulled Tomato Juice
            Pineapple Cheese-stuffed Celery

Snacker's Tomato Soup
Vegetable Slaw
Yogurt Cucumber Soup

In Chapter 5, "MILK . . . STILL THE DEPENDABLE"
Cheese Potato Salad
Pineapple Cheese Dip
Strawberry Dip

Chapter 4

BREADS WITH A
HEALTH BONUS

If you like to bake bread, your family is lucky. So are you. Homemade bread is the snack that pleases everyone. You'll enjoy trying recipes in this chapter; most of them call for whole grain flours, bran or wheat germ. And many add raisins or other fruits, for a delicious change-of-taste. Slice these homemade loaves and spread with butter for a simple snack that is hard to surpass in taste or in the good nutrition it provides. Or use bread as the logical carrier for cheese and other hearty protein snacks and sandwich fillings.

A pan of Whole Wheat Cinnamon or Pecan Rolls will generate enthusiasm on a cold day, especially if accompanied with hot cocoa. Or you might bake English Oat Muffins on your griddle, and serve them split, toasted, buttered, piping hot.

If quick breads are your forte, bake enough Sunflower Wheat Muffins or Cottage Cheese Muffins for a meal plus enough leftovers to reheat for snacks. Or try the recipes for Honey Fruit Bread and other fruited specials in this chapter. These and yeast-leavened loaves, like Mixed Grain Raisin and Whole Wheat Buttermilk Breads, make good tasting, nourishing sandwiches.

The common ingredient to all breads is flour. This may be *whole grain flour* with a minimum of milling. Or it may be *all-purpose flour,* a highly milled wheat flour which is chiefly the starch from the grain and is white and fine. (See Chapter 9, "Grocery Shopping for Good Nutrition," for more information about whole grain and enriched flours.)

The interior of grains consists largely of starch, which furnishes energy, and some protein, including gluten. Gluten is one of the important proteins in flour and has won for wheat its reputation as America's top breadmaking grain. In breadmaking, gluten is developed by kneading so that it can stretch as the yeast works and the bread rises. As it stretches, the gluten traps the leavening gas which makes the bread light. All the recipes for whole grain yeast breads in this chapter also call for some white flour to add the necessary gluten. Without it, loaves would be heavy and compact.

Dried fruits, such as dates, raisins and prunes, partially sweeten several of our recipes, thus cutting down on the sugar needed while adding flavor and nutrients.

Making breads with honey is an old country kitchen custom. For the young crowd, boosters of whole and mixed grain breads, honey is also a favorite. We chuckle at their attitude of having discovered the sweetener, as some of us remember the clover fields in bloom on the farm and how good the home-produced honey tasted. Do try our Honey Fruit Bread and Super Fruited Muffins some day soon.

Molasses, another sweetener in some of the bread recipes, has a characteristic flavor, and it also adds some iron.

Wise snack planners are sparing of sweet spreads for bread. Instead they use cheese spreads and peanut butters which are more nutritious. You'll find recipes for appetizing spreads for breads in Chapter 6. Try them on the breads you bake; your family will say snacking at your house was never better.

YEAST LEAVENED BREADS AND ROLLS

MIXED GRAIN RAISIN BREAD

Raisins and molasses sweeten loaves; orange peel and three flours add a "keep-them-guessing" flavor. Wonderful toasted

2 c. milk	2 tblsp. grated orange peel
½ c. light molasses	2 c. rye flour
¼ c. shortening	1 c. stirred whole wheat
2 tblsp. salt	flour
2½ c. all-purpose flour	1 c. raisins
2 pkgs. active dry yeast	1 c. all-purpose flour

In saucepan heat milk, molasses, shortening and salt until warm, stirring to melt shortening.

In large mixer bowl combine 2½ c. all-purpose flour, yeast and orange peel. Add warm milk mixture. Beat at low speed of mixer ½ minute, scraping sides and bottom of bowl constantly. Beat at high speed 3 minutes, scraping bowl occasionally.

By hand, stir in rye flour, whole wheat flour, raisins and enough of remaining 1 c. all-purpose flour to make a stiff dough. Turn out on lightly floured surface. Knead until smooth and elastic, about 5 minutes.

Place in greased bowl, turning to grease all sides. Cover and let rise in warm place until doubled, about 1 hour.

Punch down. Divide dough in half, cover and let rise 10 minutes. Shape each half into a loaf and place in 2 greased 9×5×3″ loaf pans. Cover and let rise in warm place until doubled, about 1 hour.

Bake in 350° oven 45 to 50 minutes or until loaves sound hollow when tapped. Remove from pans; cool on racks. Makes 2 loaves.

FOUR-GRAIN BREAD

You can cut thin, neat slices of this compact bread. The combination of grain flavors is wonderfully good

1¾ c. milk	2 pkgs. active dry yeast
¼ c. honey	1 egg
2 tblsp. shortening	¾ c. wheat germ
2 tsp. salt	¾ c. quick-cooking rolled
1 c. all-purpose flour	oats
1 c. rye flour	2 c. stirred whole wheat
½ c. buckwheat flour	flour

In saucepan heat milk, honey, shortening and salt until warm, stirring to melt shortening.

In large mixer bowl stir together all-purpose flour, rye flour, buckwheat flour and yeast. Add warm milk mixture and egg. Beat at low speed of mixer ½ minute, scraping sides and bottom of bowl constantly. Beat at high speed 3 minutes, scraping bowl occasionally.

By hand, stir in wheat germ, rolled oats and enough whole wheat flour to make a moderately stiff dough. Turn out on lightly floured surface and knead until smooth and elastic, about 10 minutes.

Place in greased bowl, turning to grease all sides. Cover and let rise in warm place until doubled, about 1 hour 15 minutes.

Punch down. Divide dough in half, cover and let rest 10 minutes. Shape each half into a loaf. Place in 2 greased 8½ ×4½ ×2½″ loaf pans. Cover and let rise in warm place until doubled, about 1 hour.

Bake in 375° oven 40 to 45 minutes or until loaves sound hollow when tapped. Remove from pans; cool on racks. Makes 2 loaves.

WHOLE WHEAT BREAD

Well-shaped loaves are larger than most whole wheat breads. Texture and taste are good; soy flour increases the protein

2¾ c. milk
½ c. vegetable oil
½ c. brown sugar, firmly
　packed
1 tblsp. salt

2 c. all-purpose flour
4 to 4½ c. stirred whole
　wheat flour
2 pkgs. active dry yeast
¾ c. stirred soy flour

In saucepan heat milk, oil, brown sugar and salt until warm.

In large mixer bowl, combine all-purpose flour, 1¾ c. whole wheat flour and yeast. Add warm milk mixture. Beat at low speed of mixer ½ minute, scraping sides and bottom of bowl constantly. Beat at high speed 3 minutes, scraping bowl occasionally.

By hand, stir in soy flour and enough remaining whole wheat flour to make a soft dough. Turn out on lightly floured surface and knead until smooth and elastic, about 5 minutes.

Place in greased bowl, turning to grease all sides. Cover and let rise in warm place until doubled, about 1 hour.

Punch down. Divide dough in half. Cover and let rest about 10 minutes. Shape each half into a loaf and place in 2 greased 9×5×3″ loaf pans. Cover and let rise in warm place until doubled, 45 to 60 minutes.

Bake in 375° oven 40 minutes or until loaves sound hollow when tapped. Remove from pans; cool on racks. Makes 2 loaves.

WHOLE WHEAT BUTTERMILK BREAD

You'll probably find the cracked wheat on cereal shelves

2½ c. buttermilk	3½ c. stirred whole wheat
¼ c. honey	flour
2 tblsp. shortening	2 pkgs. active dry yeast
1 tblsp. salt	½ tsp. baking soda
2¼ c. all-purpose flour	1 c. cracked wheat

In saucepan heat buttermilk, honey, shortening and salt until warm, stirring to melt shortening.

In large mixer bowl combine all-purpose flour, ¾ c. whole wheat flour, yeast and baking soda. Add buttermilk mixture. Beat at low speed ½ minute, scraping sides and bottom of bowl constantly. Beat at high speed 3 minutes, scraping bowl occasionally.

By hand, stir in cracked wheat and enough of the remaining whole wheat flour to make a soft dough. Turn out on lightly floured surface. Knead until elastic, about 7 minutes.

Place in greased bowl, turning to grease all sides. Cover and let rise in warm place until doubled, about 1 hour.

Punch down. Divide dough in half, cover and let rest 10 minutes. Shape each half into a loaf and place in 2 greased 8½ ×4½ ×2½″ loaf pans. Cover and let rise in warm place until doubled, or until dough has risen just above the edge of the pans, about 40 minutes.

Bake in 375° oven or until golden brown, about 35 minutes. Remove from pans; cool on racks. Makes 2 loaves.

WHOLE WHEAT PROTEIN BREAD

Wheat germ joins soy and whole wheat flours to produce this flavorful bread, high in protein with B-vitamins and iron

2½ c. milk	⅔ c. nonfat dry milk
3 tblsp. sugar	⅓ c. stirred soy flour
1 tblsp. salt	¼ c. wheat germ
2 tblsp. butter or margarine	3 to 3½ c. stirred whole
3 c. all-purpose flour	wheat flour
2 pkgs. active dry yeast	

In saucepan heat milk, sugar, salt and butter until warm, stirring to melt butter.

In large mixer bowl combine all-purpose flour and yeast. Add warm milk mixture and beat at low speed ½ minute, scraping sides and bottom of bowl constantly. Beat at high speed 3 minutes, scraping bowl occasionally.

By hand, stir in dry milk, soy flour, wheat germ and enough whole wheat flour to make a moderately soft dough. Turn out on lightly floured surface and knead until smooth and elastic, about 7 minutes.

Place in greased bowl, turning to grease all sides. Cover and let rise in warm place until doubled, 1 to 1½ hours.

Punch down. Divide dough in half, cover and let rest 10 minutes. Shape each half into a loaf and place in 2 greased 8½×4½×2½″ loaf pans. Cover and let rise in a warm place until doubled, 40 to 45 minutes.

Bake in 375° oven until golden brown, about 35 minutes. Remove from pans; cool on racks. Makes 2 loaves.

WHOLE WHEAT BRAN BREAD

Brown-crusted loaves have nutrition power—thiamin,
vitamin E, minerals—and good nutty flavor

1½ c. milk	2 c. whole bran cereal
⅓ c. butter or margarine	2 pkgs. active dry yeast
2 tblsp. light molasses	2 tblsp. sugar
2 c. all-purpose flour	2 tsp. salt
2 c. stirred whole wheat flour	2 eggs

In saucepan heat milk, butter and molasses just to warm, stirring to melt butter.

Combine all-purpose flour and whole wheat flour. Put 1 c. of this flour mixture in large mixer bowl, along with bran, yeast, sugar and salt. Add warm milk mixture and beat at low speed 2 minutes, scraping sides and bottom of bowl constantly.

Add eggs and ½ c. flour mixture; beat at high speed 2 minutes, scraping bowl occasionally.

By hand, stir in remaining flour. Turn out on lightly floured surface and knead until smooth and elastic, about 5 minutes.

Place in greased bowl, turning to grease all sides. Cover and let rise in warm place until doubled, 1 to 1½ hours.

Punch down. Divide dough in half. Shape into two balls. Place on greased baking sheet, cover and let rise in a warm place until doubled, about 1 hour.

Bake in a 375° oven 30 minutes or until loaves sound hollow when tapped. Makes 2 round loaves.

HIGH PROTEIN WHITE BREAD

Big, farm-style loaves are beautiful and taste as good as they look. No one can detect the flavor of soy flour

3 c. water	7½ to 8 c. all-purpose flour
2 tblsp. honey	¾ c. nonfat dry milk
2 tblsp. vegetable oil	2 pkgs. active dry yeast
4 tsp. salt	½ c. stirred soy flour

In saucepan, heat water, honey, oil and salt until warm.

In large mixer bowl combine 3 c. all-purpose flour, dry milk and yeast. Add warm water mixture. Beat at low speed of mixer ½ minute, scraping sides and bottom of bowl constantly. Beat at high speed 3 minutes, scraping bowl occasionally.

By hand, stir in soy flour and enough of remaining all-purpose flour to make a soft dough. Turn out on lightly floured surface and knead until smooth and elastic, 6 to 8 minutes.

Place in greased bowl, turning to grease all sides. Cover and let rise in warm place until doubled, about 1 hour.

Punch down. Divide dough in half, cover and let rest 10 minutes. Shape each half into a loaf and place in 2 greased 9×5×3″ loaf pans. Cover and let rise until doubled, 30 to 45 minutes.

Bake in 375° oven 50 to 60 minutes or until loaves sound hollow when tapped. If browning too quickly, cover with aluminum foil the last 5 to 10 minutes. Remove from pans; cool on racks. Makes 2 loaves.

PRUNE BRAN BREAD

Adding prunes to bran bread not only makes it taste good, it captures such valuables as B-vitamins and iron in loaves that also contribute bulk to the diet

1½ c. milk	5 to 5½ c. all-purpose flour
⅓ c. shortening	2 pkgs. active dry yeast
1½ c. whole bran cereal	1 tblsp. salt
1 c. cut-up cooked prunes	2 eggs
½ c. dark corn syrup	

Scald milk. Remove from heat and add shortening, stirring until it is dissolved. Stir in bran, prunes and corn syrup. Cool to warm.

In large mixer bowl combine 3 c. flour, yeast and salt. Add bran mixture and eggs. Beat at low speed ½ minute, scraping sides and bottom of bowl constantly. Beat at high speed 3 minutes, scraping bowl occasionally.

By hand stir in enough of remaining flour to make a stiff dough. Turn out on lightly floured surface. Knead until smooth and elastic, about 5 minutes.

Place in greased bowl, turning to grease all sides. Cover and let rise in a warm place until doubled, about 2 hours.

Punch down. Divide dough in half, cover and let rest 10 minutes. Shape each half into a loaf and place in 2 greased 9×5×3″ loaf pans. Cover and let rise in warm place until doubled, 1 to 1½ hours.

Bake in 350° oven 40 to 45 minutes or until loaves sound hollow when tapped. Remove from pans; cool on racks. Makes 2 loaves.

WHEAT BATTER BREAD

Beginning bread baker's favorite. Loaves bake in coffee cans

1 pkg. active dry yeast
½ c. warm water (105 to 115°)
3 tblsp. honey
1 (13 oz.) can evaporated milk
1 tsp. salt

2 tblsp. vegetable oil
2½ c. all-purpose flour
1¼ c. stirred whole wheat flour
½ c. wheat germ
¼ c. cracked wheat

Rinse large mixer bowl with warm water. Combine yeast, warm water and 1 tblsp. honey in mixer bowl. Cover and let stand in a warm place until foamy, about 20 minutes.

Add remaining 2 tblsp. honey, milk, salt, oil and all-purpose flour. Blend ½ minute at low speed of mixer, scraping sides and bottom of bowl constantly. Beat at high speed 3 minutes, scraping bowl occasionally. (Or by hand beat 300 vigorous strokes.)

By hand, beat in whole wheat flour until batter is smooth. Beat in wheat germ and cracked wheat. Scrape batter from sides of bowl. Cover and let rise in warm place until double, about 30 minutes. Stir down batter.

Spoon batter into 2 well-greased 1-pound coffee cans. Cover with greased plastic can lids. Let rise in warm place until lids pop off, 1 to 1½ hours. Remove lids.

Bake in 350° oven 45 to 50 minutes or until loaves sound hollow when tapped. Let cool in cans 10 minutes. Turn out on wire racks. Stand loaves upright to cool. Makes 2 loaves.

EASY OATMEAL BREAD

This batter bread tastes best when served warm or toasted

1¾ c. boiling water	1½ tsp. salt
¾ c. quick-cooking rolled oats	3 tblsp. vegetable oil
	4 c. all-purpose flour
¼ c. light molasses	1 pkg. active dry yeast

Pour boiling water over rolled oats. Stir in molasses, salt and oil. Cool until warm.

In large mixer bowl stir together 2 c. of the flour and yeast. Add oat mixture. Beat at low speed of mixer ½ minute, scraping sides and bottom of bowl constantly. Beat on high speed 3 minutes, scraping bowl occasionally.

By hand, stir in remaining flour until thoroughly blended. Cover and let rise in warm place until doubled, about 30 minutes. Beat 25 strokes with wooden spoon.

Spread evenly in greased 9×5×3″ loaf pan, smoothing top with buttered spatula. Let rise in warm place until 1″ from top of pan, about 20 minutes.

Bake in 425° oven 40 to 45 minutes or until loaf sounds hollow when tapped. Remove from pan, brush top of loaf with vegetable oil, if desired, and cool on rack. Makes 1 loaf.

WHOLE WHEAT BUNS

Eggs, whole wheat and enriched flours and milk fill buns with valuable nutrients. Use them to make hamburgers. Serve with tomato juice and carrot sticks for hearty snack

2 c. warm water	5 to 5½ c. all-purpose flour
½ c. sugar	2 pkgs. active dry yeast
½ c. nonfat dry milk	3 eggs
1 tblsp. salt	3½ c. stirred whole wheat flour
¾ c. vegetable oil	

In saucepan combine water, sugar, dry milk, salt and oil; heat to warm.

In large mixer bowl combine 4 c. all-purpose flour and yeast. Add warm water mixture and eggs. Beat at low speed of electric mixer ½ minute, scraping sides and bottom of bowl constantly. Beat at high speed 3 minutes, scraping bowl occasionally.

By hand, stir in whole wheat flour. Add enough remaining all-purpose flour to make a moderately soft dough. Turn out on lightly floured surface and knead until smooth and elastic, about 5 minutes.

Place in greased bowl, turning to grease all sides. Cover and let rise in warm place until doubled, 1 to 1½ hours.

Punch down. Divide dough in thirds, cover and let rest 5 minutes. Divide each portion of dough into 8 pieces. Shape into balls. Place on greased baking sheet; press balls to make 3½″ rounds. Cover; let rise until doubled, 30 to 45 minutes.

Bake in 375° oven 10 to 14 minutes or until nicely browned. Makes 24 buns.

WHOLE WHEAT SWEET ROLL DOUGH

Divide dough in half to make two kinds of rolls; recipes follow

2 c. milk	**2 pkgs. active dry yeast**
½ c. honey	**¼ c. stirred soy flour**
⅓ c. vegetable oil	**3 to 3½ c. stirred whole**
2 tsp. salt	**wheat flour**
3 c. all-purpose flour	

In saucepan combine milk, honey, oil and salt. Heat until warm.

In large mixer bowl, combine all-purpose flour and yeast. Add warm milk mixture. Beat at low speed ½ minute, scraping sides and bottom of bowl constantly. Beat at high speed 3 minutes, scraping bowl occasionally.

By hand, stir in soy flour and enough whole wheat flour to make a soft dough. Turn out on lightly floured surface and knead until smooth and elastic, about 5 minutes. Place in greased bowl, turning to grease all sides. Cover and let rise in a warm place until doubled, about 1 hour.

Punch down. Divide dough in half, and cover. Use one half for Pecan Rolls, the other half for Cinnamon Rolls.

WHOLE WHEAT CINNAMON ROLLS

If counting calories, spread warm rolls scantily with icing

½ recipe Whole Wheat Sweet Roll Dough	1 tsp. ground cinnamon
2 tblsp. butter or margarine softened	⅓ c. raisins (optional)
¼ c. sugar	Confectioners Sugar Icing (recipe follows)

Roll dough into a 15×9″ rectangle; spread with softened butter. Combine sugar and cinnamon; sprinkle over butter. Scatter raisins over sugar-cinnamon mixture. Starting at long edge, roll up like a jelly roll. Pinch edges firmly to seal well. Stretch roll if necessary to make it even thickness. Cut in 12 slices. Place rolls cut-side down in 2 greased 8″ round pans. Cover and let rise in warm place until doubled, about 45 minutes.

Bake in 375° oven 25 to 30 minutes or until nicely browned. While warm, spread with Confectioners Sugar Icing. Makes 12 rolls.

Confectioners Sugar Icing: Combine 2 c. sifted confectioners sugar, 1 tsp. vanilla and 2 tblsp. milk; heat until smooth. To save calories, cut recipe in half.

WHOLE WHEAT PECAN ROLLS

Nice to serve to guests with coffee. These rolls freeze well

½ recipe Whole Wheat Sweet Roll Dough	2 tblsp. light corn syrup
¼ c. butter or margarine melted	½ c. broken pecans
½ c. brown sugar, firmly packed	2 tblsp. butter or margarine, softened
	⅓ c. brown sugar, firmly packed

Before rolling dough, grease sides of 13×9×2" pan and pour in melted butter. Add ½ c. brown sugar, corn syrup and pecans. Spread evenly over bottom of pan.

Roll dough into a 15×9" rectangle. Spread with 2 tblsp. softened butter; sprinkle with ⅓ c. brown sugar. Starting at long edge, roll up like a jelly roll. Pinch edges firmly to seal well. Stretch roll if necessary to make it even thickness. Cut in 12 slices. Place rolls cut-side down over pecan mixture. Cover and let rise in warm place until doubled, about 45 minutes.

Bake in 375° oven 25 to 30 minutes or until nicely browned. Turn pan immediately upside down over a large tray. Let pan rest a minute before lifting off so brown sugar mixture drizzles over rolls. Makes 12 rolls.

NOTE: Freeze rolls, if desired. When frozen, wrap in aluminum foil. To serve, thaw and heat in wrapper in 325° oven about 15 minutes.

SURPRISE CLOVERLEAFS

Three bites of raisins and nuts hide in these elegant rolls

1 c. warm water (105 to
　115°)
1 pkg. active dry yeast
½ c. whole bran cereal
½ c. sugar
½ c. vegetable oil
1 tsp. salt

1 egg
1 c. rye flour
3 to 3¼ c. all-purpose
　flour
Raisin-Nut Filling (recipe
　follows)

Measure warm water into large warm bowl. Add yeast and stir to dissolve. Stir in bran cereal, sugar, oil and salt. Beat in egg, then rye flour.

Stir in enough all-purpose flour to make a moderately stiff dough. Turn out on lightly floured surface. Knead until smooth and elastic, about 5 minutes.

Place in greased bowl, turning to grease all sides. Cover and let rise in warm place until doubled, 1½ to 2 hours.

Punch down; divide dough in half. Roll out 1 portion on lightly floured surface to make 12×8″ rectangle. Cut in 24 (2″) squares. Place ½ tsp. Raisin-Nut Filling in center of each square. Wrap dough around filling and place in greased 2½″ muffin cups, 3 to a cup. Repeat with remaining half of dough. Cover and let rise in a warm place until doubled, 45 to 60 minutes.

Bake in 350° oven 15 to 20 minutes or until nicely browned. Makes 16 rolls.

Raisin-Nut Filling: Soften ⅓ c. butter or margarine, and combine with ⅓ c. brown sugar, firmly packed; 1 tsp. ground cinnamon, ⅓ c. raisins and ⅓ c. chopped nuts.

DATE OATMEAL CRESCENTS

Oats give the handsome rolls that good country kitchen taste

1 c. boiling water
1 c. quick-cooking rolled
   oats
½ c. shortening
⅓ c. brown sugar, firmly
   packed
1½ tsp. salt

1 pkg. active dry yeast
¼ c. warm water (105 to
   115°)
1 egg
3 c. all-purpose flour
Date-Nut Filling (recipe
   follows)

Pour boiling water over rolled oats. Add shortening, brown sugar and salt, stirring until shortening is melted. Cool to lukewarm.

Dissolve yeast in warm water. Beat yeast and egg into oat mixture. Gradually stir in enough flour to make a moderately stiff dough. Turn out on lightly floured surface and knead until smooth and elastic, about 5 minutes.

Place in greased bowl, turning to grease all sides. Cover and let rise in warm place until doubled, 1 to 1½ hours.

Punch down. Divide dough in thirds, and cover. Roll out 1 portion on lightly floured surface to make 12″ circle. Cut into 8 wedges. Spread a rounded teaspoonful of Date-Nut Filling along the wide edge of each wedge. Roll up, starting at wide edge. Place point-side down on greased baking sheet. Curve to form crescents. Repeat with remaining dough. Cover and let rise in warm place until doubled, about 45 minutes.

Bake in 400° oven until golden brown 10 to 13 minutes. Makes 36 rolls.

Date-Nut Filling: Thoroughly combine 1 c. chopped dates, ¾ c. chopped nuts and 1tsp. ground cinnamon.

ENGLISH OAT MUFFINS

Split, toasted and buttered is the way to feast on these muffins

1 c. boiling water
1 c. quick-cooking rolled
  oats
¼ c. brown sugar, firmly
  packed
1 tsp. salt
¼ c. vegetable oil

1 egg
1 pkg. active dry yeast
¼ c. warm water (105 to
  115°)
3 to 3½ c. all-purpose flour
Cornmeal

In large mixer bowl pour boiling water over rolled oats. Stir in brown sugar, salt and oil. Cool to lukewarm.

Dissolve yeast in warm water. Beat yeast and egg into oat mixture. Stir in enough flour to make a moderately stiff dough. Cover and let rest in warm place 30 minutes. (Dough does not double.)

Turn out on lightly floured surface and roll to ⅜" thickness. Cut into rounds with a 3" cutter. Place on greased baking sheets sprinkled with cornmeal. Cover and let rise in warm place until doubled, about 45 minutes.

Bake on lightly greased griddle over medium heat for 20 minutes, turning every 5 minutes. Makes 16 to 18 muffins.

QUICK BREADS AND MUFFINS

HONEY FRUIT BREAD

You cannot miss on flavor when you combine orange juice, dates, nuts and apples in a delicately spiced loaf. Spread moist bread with cream cheese for a nutritious snack

¼ c. orange juice
1 (8 oz.) pkg. chopped dates
2 c. sifted all-purpose flour
1½ tsp. baking powder
½ tsp. salt
½ tsp. ground cinnamon
¼ tsp. ground ginger
½ c. wheat germ

3 tblsp. butter or margarine, softened
⅔ c. honey
1 egg
½ c. dairy sour cream
1 medium apple, peeled and diced (¾ c.)
⅔ c. chopped nuts

Stir orange juice into dates; set aside.

Sift together flour, baking powder, salt, cinnamon and ginger. Stir in wheat germ.

In large mixer bowl beat together butter, honey and egg until thoroughly blended.

By hand, stir dry ingredients into honey mixture alternately with sour cream. Fold in apple, nuts and date mixture. Spread in greased 9×5×3″ loaf pan.

Bake in 350° oven 60 to 65 minutes or until cake tester, inserted in middle of loaf, comes out clean. Cool in pan 10 minutes and turn out and cool completely on wire rack. Makes 1 loaf.

PUMPKIN RAISIN LOAF

Pumpkin introduces vitamin A; whole wheat flour, nuts and raisins contribute minerals and B-vitamins. Serve open-face

2½ c. sifted all-purpose
  flour
2 tsp. baking soda
1½ tsp. salt
1 tsp. ground cinnamon
½ tsp. baking powder
¼ tsp. ground nutmeg
¼ tsp. ground cloves
1 c. stirred whole wheat
  flour

⅔ c. shortening
2½ c. sugar
4 eggs
1 (16 oz.) can pumpkin
⅔ c. water
1 c. raisins
1 c. chopped nuts

Sift together all-purpose flour, soda, salt, cinnamon, baking powder, nutmeg and cloves. Stir in whole wheat flour.

Cream together shortening and sugar until light and fluffy. Add eggs, beating until well blended.

By hand, stir in pumpkin, then water. Add dry ingredients, stirring just enough to blend well. Fold in raisins and nuts. Spread in 2 greased and floured 9×5×3″ loaf pans.

Bake in 350° oven 1 hour and 20 minutes or until cake tester, inserted in middle of loaf, comes out clean. Cool in pan 10 minutes. Turn out and cool completely on wire racks. Makes 2 loaves.

BANANA NUT BREAD

Bran adds fiber or bulk, iron and some of the B-vitamins to the loaf. Almonds are a good source of vitamin B_2 (riboflavin)

1½ c. sifted all-purpose
   flour
1 tsp. baking powder
½ tsp. baking soda
½ tsp. salt
½ tsp. ground cinnamon
1 c. whole bran cereal
1 c. mashed banana (about
   2 medium)

¼ c. buttermilk
⅓ c. butter or margarine
⅔ c. sugar
2 eggs
1 c. chopped toasted
   almonds

Sift together flour, baking powder, soda, salt and cinnamon. Stir in bran cereal.

Blend together banana and buttermilk.

Cream together butter and sugar until light and fluffy. Add eggs, beating thoroughly.

By hand, stir dry ingredients into creamed mixture alternately with banana mixture. Stir in nuts. Spread in greased and floured 8½ ×4½ ×2½″ loaf pan.

Bake in 350° oven 1 hour and 15 minutes or until cake tester, inserted in middle of loaf, comes out clean. Cool in pan 10 minutes. Turn out and cool completely on wire rack before cutting. Makes 1 loaf.

ZUCCHINI NUT BREAD

Gardener's delight—a new, nutritious, tasty way to use zucchini. Sesame seeds for topping add a bit of iron

2½ c. sifted all-purpose
    flour
¼ c. nonfat dry milk
2 tsp. baking soda
2 tsp. salt
½ tsp. baking powder
½ tsp. ground cinnamon
½ c. wheat germ
3 eggs

1 c. vegetable oil
1 c. sugar
1 c. brown sugar, firmly
    packed
1 tsp. vanilla
2 c. grated zucchini
1 c. chopped nuts
2 tblsp. sesame seeds

Sift together flour, dry milk, baking soda, salt, baking powder and cinnamon. Stir in wheat germ.

In mixer bowl combine eggs, oil, sugars and vanilla. Beat at high speed until thick and foamy.

By hand, stir in zucchini. Add dry ingredients, stirring just enough to moisten. Fold in nuts.

Spread in 2 greased and floured 8½×4½×2½″ loaf pans. Sprinkle tops with sesame seeds.

Bake in 350° oven 65 to 75 minutes or until cake tester, inserted in middle of loaf, comes out clean. (Tops will not be smooth.) Cool in pans 10 minutes. Turn out and cool completely on wire racks. Makes 2 loaves.

SUPER FRUITED MUFFINS

One muffin supplies the snacker about one fourth of his daily requirement of complete protein. Muffins have fine flavor and good texture. Perfect to serve with milk

1¼ c. stirred soy flour	¾ c. orange juice
⅔ c. nonfat dry milk	2 tblsp. honey
2 tsp. baking powder	2 tblsp. vegetable oil
½ tsp. salt	½ c. chopped dates
¼ tsp. ground cinnamon	¼ c. chopped nuts
2 eggs	½ tsp. grated orange peel

Sift together soy flour, dry milk, baking powder, salt and cinnamon.

Beat eggs slightly. Beat in orange juice, honey and oil. Stir in dates, nuts and orange peel.

Add egg-date mixture to dry ingredients, stirring just enough to moisten. Spoon into 12 greased 2½" muffin cups.

Bake in 350° oven 25 minutes or until browned. Makes 12 muffins.

BRAN RAISIN MUFFINS

To reheat leftover muffins for a wholesome snack, wrap in foil or place in paper bag and warm in a slow oven

1 c. sifted all-purpose flour	½ c. raisins
2 tsp. baking powder	⅓ c. shortening
1 tsp. salt	½ c. sugar
½ tsp. baking soda	1 egg
3 c. whole bran cereal	1 c. buttermilk

Sift together flour, baking powder, salt and baking soda. Stir in bran cereal and raisins.

Cream together shortening and sugar until light and fluffy. Add egg and beat thoroughly.

Add dry ingredients alternately with buttermilk, stirring just enough to moisten (batter will be lumpy). Spoon into 12 greased 2½" muffin cups.

Bake in 400° oven 20 to 25 minutes or until browned. Remove from pan. Serve hot. Makes 12 muffins.

CINNAMON PEAR MUFFINS

To make these ahead, bake, cool muffins on racks, return to muffin pans, cover with foil and freeze. To serve, reheat without thawing or uncovering in a 325° to 350° oven

2 c. sifted all-purpose flour	1 c. snipped dried pears
3 tsp. baking powder	1 tsp. grated orange peel
1 tsp. salt	2 tblsp. sugar
¼ c. sugar	¼ to ½ tsp. ground
1 egg, beaten	cinnamon
1 c. milk	
¼ c. butter or margarine, melted	

Sift together flour, baking powder and salt into a bowl. Stir in ¼ c. sugar.

Combine egg, milk and melted butter.

Make a well in dry ingredients. Add egg mixture, stirring just enough to moisten (batter will be lumpy). Fold in pears and orange peel. Spoon into 12 greased 2½" muffin cups. Combine remaining 2 tblsp. sugar with cinnamon and sprinkle on tops of muffins.

Bake in 400° oven 20 to 25 minutes or until browned. Cool 5 minutes before removing from pan. Serve warm with butter. Makes 12 muffins.

SUNFLOWER WHEAT MUFFINS

Muffins have pleasing, nutlike, wheat taste. Sunflower seeds contain oil, protein, some B-vitamins and iron

¾ c. sifted all-purpose flour	1 egg, beaten
2½ tsp. baking powder	¾ c. milk
½ tsp. salt	⅓ c. vegetable oil
1¼ c. stirred whole wheat flour	⅓ c. honey
½ c. coarsely chopped, roasted sunflower seeds	

Sift together all-purpose flour, baking powder and salt. Stir in whole wheat flour and sunflower seeds.

Blend together egg, milk, oil and honey.

Make a well in dry ingredients. Add egg mixture, stirring just enough to moisten (batter will be lumpy). Spoon into 12 greased 2½" muffin cups.

Bake in 400° oven 20 to 25 minutes or until browned. Makes 12 muffins.

COTTAGE CHEESE MUFFINS

Remember the snackers. Cool and freeze leftover muffins. To reheat any number of frozen muffins, wrap them in foil and heat without thawing in 350° oven 25 minutes

1½ c. sifted all-purpose flour	½ c. stirred whole wheat flour
¼ c. sugar	2 eggs
4 tsp. baking powder	1 c. small-curd creamed cottage cheese
1 tsp. salt	
½ tsp. baking soda	1 c. buttermilk
1 c. cornmeal	⅓ c. vegetable oil

Sift together all-purpose flour, sugar, baking powder, salt and soda. Stir in cornmeal and whole wheat flour.

In small bowl beat eggs; stir in cottage cheese, buttermilk and oil.

Make a well in dry ingredients. Add egg mixture, stirring just enough to moisten (batter will be lumpy). Spoon into 24 greased 2½″ muffin cups.

Bake in 400° oven until browned, 20 to 23 minutes. Makes 24 muffins.

FREEZER FRENCH TOAST

Try to slice bread evenly so it will absorb egg mixture uniformly. A pleasing way to get eggs, bread and milk

4 eggs
1 c. milk
8 slices day-old French bread, cut ¾″ thick
Melted butter or margarine

Beat eggs slightly; beat in milk. Dip bread slices on both sides in egg mixture. Place in 15×10×1″ jelly roll pan. Pour remaining egg mixture over bread. Let stand several minutes. Turn and let stand until all egg mixture is absorbed. Freeze, uncovered, until firm. Pack in plastic bag and store in freezer. Makes 8 slices.

To serve, place as many slices of bread as desired on buttered baking sheet. Brush with melted butter. Bake at once in 500° oven 8 minutes. Turn slices; brush with melted butter. Continue baking 6 minutes, or until browned on both sides. Serve with honey, table syrup or jam.

FROZEN WHEAT WAFFLES

With these in the freezer, waffles are easy as toast

1 c. sifted all-purpose flour
¾ c. stirred whole wheat
  flour
1 tsp. baking powder
1 tsp. baking soda
½ tsp. salt
2 eggs
⅓ c. vegetable oil
2 c. buttermilk

In large bowl stir together all-purpose flour, whole wheat flour, baking powder, soda and salt. Make well in dry ingredients. Add eggs, oil and buttermilk. Beat until well blended.

Bake in preheated waffle iron; cool. Place waxed paper between waffles, wrap and freeze.

To serve, heat frozen waffles in toaster. Or spread them out on baking sheet and bake, uncovered, in 325° oven 15 minutes. Makes 3 (10″) square waffles or 7 (7″) round waffles.

Milk and milk products are important ingredients in other recipes in this book; consult Index for page numbers.

In Chapter 2, "SNACK BUT STAY SLIM"
            Blueberry Sicles
            Butterscotch Pumpkin Pudding
            Diet Apricot Dessert
            Dilly Cheese-stuffed Celery
            French Onion Dip
            Low-Cal Clam Dip
            Peaches with Spicy Yogurt
            Pineapple Cheese-stuffed Celery
            Raspberry Pops
            Slim Jim Cheeseburgers
            Strawberry Buttermilk Sherbet

Tuna Nibblers
Tuna Salad Sandwiches
Yogurt Cucumber Soup
Zesty Cheese Dip

In Chapter 3, "FRUITS AND VEGETABLES"
Blue Cheese Tomatoes
Frosty Orange Nog
Fruit-Yogurt Combo
Orange-Ice Cream Pops
Tropical Fruit Shake

In Chapter 4, "BREADS WITH A HEALTH BONUS"
Cottage Cheese Muffins

In Chapter 6, "SUBSTANTIAL SNACKS"
Bologna Cheesewiches
Braunschweiger Dip
Hamburger Pizzas
Luncheon Meat Cheese Sandwiches
Pizza Muffins
Reuben Sandwich Filling
Sausage Pizzas
Snackers' Casseroles
Stuffed Frankfurters
Tacos

In Chapter 7, "SWEETS TO EAT"
Pineapple Cheese Pie

Chapter 5

MILK . . . STILL THE DEPENDABLE

Milk and milk products are a primary route to snacks for good health. You can serve these foods plain—few people will reject a glass of cool milk, a dish of ice cream or crackers and cheese. But there are many interesting, new snacks with appetite appeal that feature dairy foods. This chapter presents a sampler of recipes for such homemade treats. Many other recipes including dairy products as ingredients will be found throughout this book (see list at end of this chapter).

Tell your husband you've got Potted Cheese in the refrigerator. When he wants to invite a farm visitor in for coffee, it makes a satisfying snack spread on rye bread or crackers, and the men can help themselves. Keep frozen orange juice and vanilla ice cream in the freezer for your teen-ager to whip up luscious Orange Slush when he has special company. Serve delicately spiced Strawberry Dip with fruit and melon dippers to the calorie-counting members of your bridge club on a hot morning. Whirl Old-Fashioned Eggnog or Vanilla Milk Shake with the blender to treat the preschool children.

As these recipes demonstrate, milk and milk products are superb mixers. That they combine beautifully with many kinds of foods aids the snack planner. And the nutritional contribution they make to any such combination is as excellent as the taste.

One of their virtues is the calcium they contain. Without using milk and milk products in our daily diets, it is almost impossible to meet our nutritional requirements for the essential mineral calcium, and also for the vitamin riboflavin. By choosing them for between meal enjoyment, you relieve the three regular meals of the load to furnish enough calcium.

The protein in the milk foods is of the highest quality. (Milk gives you what nutritionists call "complete" protein; like meat, it contains the eight amino acids which the body cannot make by itself.) That means that even a small amount of milk with its high quality protein increases the value of the protein you get from cereal sources.

Whenever you are fixing a snack that needs more protein and flavor, consider adding a little cheese. Many mothers have adopted this habit to the benefit of their families. For example, tuck a slice of cheese in a sandwich (see Cheesy Fishburgers). Sprinkle grated or shredded cheese on a bowl of steaming hot soup. Cut cheese in slender strips and toss them in the green salad. You will find in this book many other ways to include cheese in snacks. It is healthful and makes snacks taste extra good.

Please family and friends by topping desserts with ice cream. Apple Torte with such a topping tastes twice as good.

Remember when you are adding cheese and ice cream, you are also adding calories. Be sure your snackers need this extra energy and that it will not contribute to their gaining unwanted weight. It might be helpful to know what the calorie differences are in the different forms of milk and milk products. Here are the figures that will guide you:

1 cup whole milk	160 calories
1 cup skim milk	90 calories
1 cup "two per cent" milk	145 calories
1 cup buttermilk	90 calories
½ cup yogurt	60 calories
½ cup cottage cheese	85 calories
1 ounce Cheddar type cheese	70 calories
1 ounce cream cheese	105 calories
½ cup ice cream	130 calories

MILK DRINKS AND DESSERTS

HOMEMADE ICE CREAM SODA

Milk and ice cream add nutrients to the bottled soft drink

½ c. milk
2 tblsp. chocolate syrup
1 scoop vanilla ice cream
    (½ c.)

**Lemon-lime carbonated
beverage**

Combine milk and syrup in 8 oz. glass. Add ice cream. Pour in carbonated beverage to fill glass. Makes 1 serving.

OLD-FASHIONED EGGNOG

If you don't have a recipe for the traditional drink, try this version chilled with ice. Children with no appetite for breakfast often welcome it

1 c. milk
1 egg
1 tblsp. sugar

¼ tsp. vanilla
½ c. crushed ice (optional)

Combine all ingredients in blender container. Cover and whirl until smooth. Makes 1 serving.

NOTE: Use only clean, whole (not cracked) eggs in eggnog or any recipe calling for eggs which will not be cooked.

SUPER STRAWBERRY MALT

Fine way to use berries from your freezer. For fewer calories, substitute ice milk for ice cream

1½ c. milk
1 (10 oz.) pkg. frozen
   strawberries, partially
   thawed

1 pt. vanilla or strawberry
   ice cream
¼ c. malted milk mix

Combine all ingredients in blender container. Cover and whirl just until blended. Makes about 1 quart.

ORANGE SLUSH

Youngsters and grownups alike enjoy this luscious drink. Orange juice adds vitamin C, ice cream contributes calcium and protein

1½ c. orange juice
1 pt. vanilla ice cream

Combine ingredients in blender container. Cover and whirl just until blended. Makes 2½ cups.

GRAPE FROST

When craving a sweet snack, avoid one filled with empty calories. Make this delightful combination of ice cream, fruit juice and milk. The drink is very thick

¼ c. milk
2 tblsp. frozen grape juice
  concentrate, thawed

1 tblsp. frozen orange juice
  concentrate, thawed
1 pt. vanilla ice cream

Combine all ingredients in blender container. Cover and whirl until smooth. Makes 1½ cups or 2 servings.

NOTE: You may want to skip dessert in the evening meal if you serve Grape Frost in midafternoon.

MEXICAN CHOCOLATE

The cinnamon taste is faint; add more spice if you prefer

1 qt. milk
2 (3″) cinnamon sticks
5 (1 oz.) squares semisweet chocolate

Combine ingredients in saucepan. Cook and stir over medium heat until chocolate is melted and mixture just comes to a boil. Remove from heat and let stand at least 15 minutes. (Or cool and chill.)

Reheat at serving time, removing cinnamon sticks when beverage is scalding hot. Beat vigorously with rotary beater until foamy. Serve immediately. Makes 6 servings.

CHOCOLATE PEPPERMINT SHAKE

With a blender, you can make six shakes all at once

2 c. milk
½ c. chocolate syrup
1 qt. peppermint stick ice cream

Combine milk and chocolate syrup in blender container. Spoon in ice cream. Cover and whirl until smooth. Makes 5½ cups or 6 servings.

CHOCOLATE BANANA SHAKE

Hearty, nourishing special that really pleases children

½ c. milk
½ banana, cut in chunks
½ c. chocolate ice cream

Combine ingredients in blender container. Cover and whirl until blended. Makes 1 serving.

VANILLA MILK SHAKE

Marvelous snack for an underweight youngster or adult. It is richer and sweeter than traditional eggnogs

2 c. milk   **1 egg (optional)**
1 pt. vanilla ice cream   **1 tsp. vanilla**

Combine all ingredients in blender container. Cover and whirl just until smooth. Makes 3 cups.

NOTE: Use only clean, whole (not cracked) eggs in shakes or any recipe calling for eggs which will not be cooked.

DOUBLE CHOCOLATE SHAKE

Rich, special-occasion snack that gets an enthusiastic reception

2 c. skim milk
½ c. chocolate syrup
1 pt. chocolate ice cream

Combine all ingredients in blender container. Cover and whirl just until blended. Makes 1 quart.

STRAWBERRY DIP

Serve this cool dip with chilled fruit on a sultry afternoon

¼ tsp. ground cinnamon
1 (8 oz.) carton strawberry flavor yogurt
Assorted fruit and melon dippers

Stir cinnamon into yogurt. Serve with fruit pieces on wooden picks: unpeeled apple wedges, banana chunks, green grapes, pineapple chunks, cantaloupe and honeydew melon balls. Makes 1 cup.

HIGH-HAT BANANA CUSTARDS

This delightful milk and egg dessert tastes like banana cream pie, but with no crust there are fewer calories.

¾ c. sugar
¼ c. flour
½ tsp. salt
3 egg yolks
1 egg
1½ c. milk

1 tsp. vanilla
1 large banana, sliced thin
3 egg whites
¼ tsp. cream of tartar
6 tblsp. sugar

Combine ¾ c. sugar, flour and salt.

In heavy saucepan beat egg yolks and 1 egg. Blend in milk, then dry ingredients. Cook over low heat, stirring constantly, until mixture is very thick. Remove from heat and stir in vanilla. Cool.

For each dessert, measure out ⅓ c. custard. Pour half of it into 6 oz. custard cup. Top with 4 or 5 banana slices, then with remaining custard. Repeat to fill 5 more custard cups.

Combine egg whites and cream of tartar. Beat until frothy. Add remaining 6 tblsp. sugar, 1 tblsp. at a time, beating until mixture is glossy and forms very stiff peaks. Spoon over each custard, sealing to edges of cup.

Bake in 350° oven 10 to 12 minutes or until nicely browned. Makes 6 servings.

STRAWBERRY ANGEL DESSERT

Pretty, colorful and tasty dessert to serve afternoon or evening guests. You can use plain yogurt if you prefer; it has about half the calories of flavored yogurt

1 c. strawberry flavor yogurt
4 slices angel food cake
1 (10 oz.) pkg. frozen strawberries, thawed

Spoon ¼ c. yogurt over each cake slice. Top with strawberries. Makes 4 servings.

MAPLE CUSTARD

Serve this thrifty custard between meals. It also pinch-hits as a nutritious breakfast for people in a hurry

1 c. nonfat dry milk   **1½ c. maple flavor syrup**
2½ c. water   **1 tsp. vanilla**
4 eggs

In saucepan combine dry milk and water; heat to scalding. Remove from heat.

Beat eggs slightly, stir in syrup and vanilla. Slowly pour hot milk into egg mixture, stirring constantly.

Strain into 8 (5 oz.) custard cups. Place cups in 13×9×2″ pan on oven rack and pour hot water into pan to 1″ depth.

Bake in 325° oven 45 to 50 minutes, or until knife inserted off center comes out clean. Remove from pan. Serve warm or chilled. To chill, cover warm custards with plastic wrap and refrigerate. Makes 8 custards.

APPLE TORTE

Thanks to its ice cream topping, this dessert has superb flavor. Valuable nutrients include protein, calcium, iron, trace minerals and some B-vitamins . . . a healthful treat for friends who come for an evening visit

1 c. sugar
½ c. sifted all-purpose flour
2 tsp. baking powder
4 c. diced, unpeeled tart
   apples
½ c. chopped dates
½ c. raisins

½ c. chopped nuts
1 tblsp. butter or margarine,
   melted
1 egg, beaten
1 tsp. vanilla
Vanilla ice cream

In large mixing bowl thoroughly combine all ingredients except ice cream. Do not beat. Spread in greased 8″ square pan. Bake in 400° oven until apples are done, 40 to 45 minutes.

Serve warm or cold. Cut in squares and top each serving with vanilla ice cream. Makes 6 to 8 servings.

CHEESE DIPS, SPREADS, SANDWICHES

PINEAPPLE CHEESE DIP

Easy, luscious and different way to serve fruits with cheese

1 (8½ oz.) can crushed
　pineapple
1 (5 oz.) jar Neufchatel
　cheese spread with
　pimiento

Apple slices
Banana chunks
Melon balls
Strawberries

Drain pineapple, reserving liquid. Beat cheese spread until smooth. Stir in crushed pineapple and 2 tblsp. of reserved pineapple juice. Serve as a dip for fruit. Makes 1¼ cups.

DILLED CHEESE DIP

Extra special with cucumber and other raw vegetable strips

1 (8 oz.) pkg. Neufchatel
　cheese, softened
½ c. plain yogurt

¾ tsp. salt
¼ tsp. dried dill weed

In small bowl, beat cheese with electric mixer at medium speed until smooth and fluffy. Beat in remaining ingredients. Serve as a dip with raw vegetables. Makes 1¼ cups.

POTTED CHEESE
(First Week)

Makes a superb spread for crackers and good sandwich filling

1 lb. sharp Cheddar cheese	1 tsp. Worcestershire sauce
1 (3 oz.) pkg. cream cheese	2 tblsp. vegetable oil
1 tsp. dry mustard	1 tblsp. milk
1 tsp. garlic salt	

Grate Cheddar cheese into large mixer bowl. Let grated and cream cheeses stand at room temperature just long enough to soften. Add remaining ingredients. Beat at low speed until blended thoroughly. Pack into jar, cover and refrigerate at least 24 hours before using. Makes 3 cups.

POTTED CHEESE
(Second Week)

Use remnants of cheese spread as starter to replenish pot

Remnants in cheese pot	2 tsp. vegetable oil
1 c. shredded Monterey	¼ tsp. Worcestershire sauce
Jack, Swiss or Cheddar	⅛ tsp. dry mustard
cheese	⅛ tsp. garlic salt
2 tsp. milk	

Let cheese pot remnants stand at room temperature just long enough to soften.

Place Monterey Jack, Swiss or Cheddar cheese, milk, oil and seasonings in small mixer bowl and let warm to room temperature. Beat with milk, oil and seasonings until blended. Beat in remnants from cheese pot. Return to jar, cover and refrigerate 24 hours before using.

You can replenish the cheese spread for several weeks, adding the kind of cheese and the amount of it you like. Add enough milk and oil to make potted cheese of spreading consistency and seasonings to make it flavorful.

ZIPPY BEEF DIP

For a low-calorie dip to serve with raw vegetable dippers, make this attractive, peppy, protein and calcium special

1 c. small-curd creamed cottage cheese	1½ tblsp. horseradish
	1 tblsp. chopped onion
2 tblsp. skim milk	1 (2½ oz.) jar dried beef,
2 tblsp. minced parsley	coarsely shredded

Combine all ingredients in blender. Blend at low speed until beef is evenly shredded and distributed throughout cheese mixture. Chill, covered, at least ½ hour to blend flavors. Serve with raw vegetable dippers. Makes 1⅓ cups.

PARMESAN TUNA DIP

Among high quality protein foods, tuna is one of the best budget stretchers. In this dip, Parmesan cheese adds a bit more protein and helps promote the distinctive Italian flavor

1 c. dairy sour cream	2 tblsp. lemon juice
1 (3¼ oz.) can tuna, drained and flaked	2 tsp. dry Italian salad dressing mix
⅓ c. grated Parmesan cheese	Chopped parsley (optional)
	Assorted vegetable dippers
1 hard-cooked egg, chopped	

Combine all ingredients except parsley and vegetable dippers. Cover and chill. To serve, spoon into bowl and garnish with parsley. Place on a tray and surround with raw vegetable dippers, such as sticks of zucchini, carrots, celery and cucumber, cauliflowerets and green onions. Makes 1½ cups.

TUNA-CREAM CHEESE SPREAD

Three ounces tuna furnish one third of the daily protein requirement. Chill this sandwich spread and let your family enjoy snacking on it. It pleases people of all ages

1 (7 oz.) can tuna, drained and flaked

2 hard-cooked eggs, chopped

¼ c. chopped celery

2 tblsp. finely chopped dill pickle

1 tblsp. finely chopped green onion

1 (3 oz.) pkg. cream cheese, softened

2 tblsp. mayonnaise or salad dressing

1 tsp. lemon juice

Combine tuna, eggs, celery, pickle and onion.

Blend together cream cheese, mayonnaise and lemon juice. Stir into tuna mixture. Cover and chill. Serve with rye bread or toast. Makes 1¾ cups.

PARTY TUNA SPREAD

An elegant spread to serve to evening guests with crisp whole wheat crackers or party rye bread

½ c. butter or margarine, softened

1 (8 oz.) pkg. cream cheese, softened

2 (7 oz.) cans tuna, drained

2 tblsp. chopped green onion

1 tblsp. lemon juice

1 tblsp. capers

¼ tsp. salt

¼ tsp. dried tarragon

¼ c. chopped parsley

Paprika

Crackers or rye bread

Cream together butter and cream cheese. Stir in tuna, onion, lemon juice, capers, salt and tarragon. Shape in mound on serving plate. Sprinkle with parsley and paprika. Chill. Makes about 3 cups.

EASY NACHOS

Beans and cheese together add up to top quality protein. These tidbits, favorites in the Southwest, are quick to fix

24 taco-flavored tortilla chips
½ c. canned bean dip
½ c. shredded Cheddar cheese (2 oz.)

Place chips on broiler pan. Top each chip with 1 tsp. bean dip, then with cheese. Broil 4" from heat until cheese melts, 1 to 3 minutes. Makes 24.

COTTAGE CHEESE SANDWICHES

Cottage cheese has fewer calories than other members of the cheese family. Calcium and protein are its main nutrients. Substitute lettuce for toast and you have a good salad

1½ c. small-curd creamed
cottage cheese (12 oz.)
½ c. shredded carrots
¼ c. finely chopped celery
2 tblsp. chopped green
onion
¼ tsp. salt
¼ tsp. dried dill weed
6 slices buttered whole
wheat toast
Thin tomato slices
(optional)

Combine cottage cheese, carrots, celery, onion, salt and dill weed. Cover and store in refrigerator at least 30 minutes before using. Chilled mixture will keep a couple of days.

When ready to make sandwich, lay tomato slice, if desired, on toast slice. Top with ⅓ c. cottage cheese mixture. Makes 6 open-face sandwiches.

GRILLED TORTILLA SANDWICHES

Corn is soaked in lime water before grinding into cornmeal to make tortillas. Some particles of lime adhere to meal, adding calcium. Sandwiches are teen-age favorites

1 (9 oz.) pkg. frozen
   tortillas, thawed (12)
6 tblsp. butter or margarine
   softened

6 oz. Monterey Jack cheese,
   sliced ⅛″ thick
2 tblsp. chopped canned
   green chilies

For each sandwich, spread one side of tortilla with butter. Place butter side down in skillet. Cook until lightly browned. Cover with cheese slices; sprinkle with 1 tsp. chopped chilies. Butter second tortilla and place over cheese, butter side up. Turn immediately. Cook until second side is lightly browned and cheese is melted. Makes 6 sandwiches.

NOTE: If making only one sandwich at a time, store remaining tortillas in refrigerator.

CHEESY FISHBURGER

Cheese not only steps up appeal and taste of this quick hot sandwich, but adds calcium to the diet

1 portion frozen breaded
   fish
Vegetable oil
1 slice process American
   cheese

1 hamburger bun, split
Golden Tartar Sauce (recipe
   follows)

In small skillet, cook fish in hot oil until golden brown on one side, about 3 minutes. Turn and top with cheese slice cut to fit fish. Continue cooking until golden brown on other side, about 2 minutes. Place in split hamburger bun and top generously with Golden Tartar Sauce. Makes 1 serving.

GOLDEN TARTAR SAUCE

Use at least one tablespoon of sauce per sandwich

1 c. mayonnaise or salad
   dressing
½ c. sweet pickle relish

1½ tsp. prepared mustard
1 tsp. grated onion

Combine all ingredients. Cover and refrigerate. Sauce will keep a week or two. Makes about 1½ cups.

HAM AND CHEESE MUFFINS

These open-face sandwiches heat while the coffee is brewing

1 c. process American
   cheese spread
1 c. finely cubed,
   fully-cooked ham

½ tsp. dry mustard
¼ tsp. Worcestershire sauce
4 English muffins, split
Butter or margarine

Combine cheese spread, ham, mustard and Worcestershire sauce. Butter English muffin halves completely to edges and spread cheese mixture evenly over each half. Place on baking sheet and freeze. When frozen, store in plastic bag.

To serve, place the desired number of unthawed sandwiches on a baking sheet. Bake in 475° oven 10 to 12 minutes. Makes 8 sandwiches.

CHEESE POTATO SALAD

Cheese and eggs convert a top vegetable salad into a superior main dish; green beans, onions and pepper brighten it with color. Cook potatoes in jackets to conserve vitamins and minerals. A big recipe—there will be leftovers for snackers

4 to 5 medium potatoes	¾ c. chopped celery
2 tblsp. vinegar	⅓ c. chopped green onion
½ tsp. salt	¼ c. chopped green pepper
¼ tsp. pepper	1½ c. mayonnaise or salad
1 lb. Swiss cheese, cut in	dressing
¼" cubes	2 tblsp. vinegar
3 hard-cooked eggs,	2 tblsp. prepared mustard
chopped	1½ tsp. salt
1 (16 oz.) can green beans,	
drained	

Cook potatoes in jackets; let cool slightly. Peel and cube warm potatoes (should have about 4 c.); toss with 2 tblsp. vinegar, ½ tsp. salt and pepper. Cool.

Add cheese, eggs, beans, celery, onion and green pepper.

Combine mayonnaise, 2 tblsp. vinegar, mustard and 1½ tsp. salt. Gently stir into potato mixture. Chill thoroughly. Makes about 9 cups.

MEXICAN CHEESEBURGERS

Meat mixture may be made ahead and stored in the refrigerator

1 lb. ground beef	½ tsp. chili powder
½ c. chopped onion	¼ tsp. cumin
½ c. chopped green pepper	8 slices process American
1 (8 oz.) can tomato sauce	cheese
1 tsp. salt	8 tortillas

In skillet, cook ground beef with onion and green pepper until meat is browned. Add tomato sauce, salt, chili powder and cumin. Cook and stir until meat absorbs most of sauce. Use immediately or cool, cover and refrigerate.

Reheat beef mixture when ready to serve. For each cheeseburger, place a slice of cheese on a tortilla. Top with hot beef mixture and roll up. Makes 8 servings.

NOTE: Meat mixture is milder in flavor than most Mexican food. More chili powder may be added.

Chapter 6

SUBSTANTIAL SNACKS FOR MEAL-MISSERS

Families still meet around the table for meals—but it's not the everyday, everyone-on-time occasion that it used to be. The pressures of field work may delay farmers, while after school jobs or basketball or band practice may put high schoolers on different schedules. You yourself may be drafted for community or church work.

Every family has days (sometimes weeks) when there's a vacant chair at the table . . . or when everyone seems to be meeting each other coming and going.

There's little you can do about the irregular schedules, but as guardian of your family's health you can provide for these times, rather than let them create a gap in your family's food intake.

The children will be more likely to come home if there is some good quick food *ready*, and you'll be happier if you don't have to be on call at the stove seven times a day. To accomplish this will take some planning on your part, and then informing your husband and children what you've put in the freezer or refrigerator, for them to assemble or heat and eat. If you let them help you prepare and package the food, you'll be sure they'll know how to fix it later.

Every recipe that follows in this chapter calls for ingredients that supply high quality protein. Many of them also supply important minerals and vitamins. Anything you can do to substitute this type of mini-meal for the popular packaged snacks which are likely to be high in calories and low in nutrients, will contribute to good health.

Microwave ovens miraculously step up the speed for heating food from the freezer for off-hour eating. Women who own this appliance say it's wonderful to be able to have a hot meal ready for a latecomer only minutes after he walks in the door. Recipes in this chapter give directions for both microwave and conventional heating.

For off-hour eating, start with our hearty sandwiches. They are great favorites of teen-agers. And all of them hold good protein foods, such as meats, cheese, fish, baked beans. You can make most of the sandwiches ahead at your convenience and store them, individually wrapped, in the freezer ready to heat. Or you can thaw them in the refrigerator to eat cold. Warm or cold, a food provides the same nutrients—so don't worry too much about cold meals.

If there is a jar of refrigerator salad on hand, it is easy to spoon some of it out to accompany a sandwich. (For recipes, see Chapter 3, Fruits and Vegetables.) That is a fast way to build a good two-piece meal. Add a glass of milk, tomato juice or fruit juice and you have a three-piece menu of merit.

In this chapter check the recipes for Chicken and Italian Vegetable Soups and those for miniature casseroles, like Ground Beef Mini-Meals and Individual Chicken Casseroles. They are typical of the tasty main-dish snacks that supply both vegetables and meat.

You will notice that both the soups and casserole mixtures are frozen in small amounts. They are large enough for a serving—

but you can always heat two if you're feeding a hungry teen-ager or a physically active person.

Young people also like to fix their own snacks especially if it involves using a portable electric appliance like the toaster-oven, skillet or grill. And the blender, of course, has no peer for fixing beverages.

Pizzas retain great popularity. Once you make our Individual Pizza Crusts, easy Homemade Pizza Sauce and Hamburger and Sausage Pizzas, you will understand why they create so much enthusiasm among teens.

Tacos, borrowed from Mexican snackers, are gaining wide acceptance, too. You can keep the meat filling and shredded cheese in the refrigerator and taco shells nearby in the cupboard. Teens like to fill their own and most snackers will take time to chop a little lettuce to top the pocket sandwiches.

Grownups sometimes are odd-hour eaters—especially farmer husbands. With Reuben Sandwich Filling on hand, many a man is happy to fix himself a quick sandwich for a hearty snack. But this chapter was also written for the woman who lunches alone and thinks she cannot spare time to prepare a meal. Keeping the makings handy removes the temptation to meal-skipping. And a stock of quick snack ingredients on hand enables you to serve someone in the family or a friend something tasty and satisfying—and healthful—to eat in a hurry.

HEARTY SANDWICHES

SECOND-TIME SANDWICH

Meat and cheese sandwiches make the best second-show snacks

1 leftover sandwich	1 tblsp. milk
1 egg	1 tblsp. butter or margarine

Remove lettuce and tomatoes from sandwich if it contains them, wrap in foil or plastic wrap and store in refrigerator up to 2 days.

Beat together egg and milk. Dip sandwich on both sides in egg mixture, letting it stand until all of mixture is absorbed.

Melt butter in small skillet and cook sandwich over medium heat, turning to brown on both sides. Makes 1 sandwich.

REUBEN SANDWICH FILLING

With a Reuben container in your refrigerator, hungry people can make a hot nourishing sandwich in minutes

1 (12 oz.) can corned beef, chopped	¾ c. mayonnaise or salad dressing
8 oz. shredded Swiss cheese (2 c.)	3 tblsp. chili sauce
1 (16 oz.) can sauerkraut, drained and snipped	Rye bread
	Butter or margarine

Combine corned beef, cheese, sauerkraut, mayonnaise and chili sauce. Cover and store in refrigerator.

To serve, spread filling between rye bread slices. Butter outside of bread slices. Cook on sandwich grill or in skillet until cheese melts. Makes about 5 cups.

LIVERWURST REUBENS

Liverwurst provides iron and it's easy to heat these favorites

16 slices rye bread	1 (6 oz.) pkg. sliced Swiss cheese
Prepared mustard	
1 lb. liverwurst	Butter or margarine, softened
1 (16 oz.) can sauerkraut	

To make each sandwich, spread rye bread with mustard, then with liverwurst. Top with drained sauerkraut and cheese cut to fit sandwich. Spread second slice of rye bread with mustard and lay mustard side down on cheese. Butter both sides of sandwich.

Cook in skillet, electric toaster oven or on sandwich grill until both sides are browned and cheese is melted. Makes 8 sandwiches.

MARINATED SAUSAGE SANDWICHES

Get this sandwich filling ready when you expect several snackers. It's easy to finish sandwiches while coffee perks

½ c. vegetable oil
⅓ c. vinegar
1 tblsp. chopped parsley
½ tsp. salt
½ tsp. dried basil
¼ tsp. pepper
1½ lbs. Polish sausage, cooked and cut in ¼″ slices

3 peeled tomatoes, thinly sliced
½ medium onion, sliced and separated in rings
12 slices Italian or rye bread

Combine oil, vinegar, parsley, salt, basil and pepper in 12×8×2″ baking dish. Add sliced sausage, tomatoes and onion. Toss gently to coat sausage and vegetables. Cover and refrigerate at least 4 hours, stirring occasionally. Serve drained sausage mixture on bread slices, open-face style. Makes 12 sandwiches.

LUNCHEON MEAT CHEESE SANDWICHES

For "hero dogs" use long hard rolls instead of hot dog buns

8 hot dog buns, split　　　　**1 (6 oz.) pkg. sliced**
Butter or margarine　　　　　　**mozzarella cheese**
6 slices salami
6 slices chopped ham
　luncheon meat

Butter bun halves completely to edges. Cut salami and lunch-eon meat slices in thirds, cheese slices in fourths crosswise. Place 2 pieces of each between bun halves. Wrap sandwiches individually in aluminum foil, using drugstore wrap. Freeze.

To serve, place frozen, wrapped sandwich in unheated oven. Turn oven to 425° and bake 30 minutes. Or let wrapped sandwiches thaw in refrigerator and eat cold. Makes 8 sandwiches.

To Use Microwave Oven: Toast bun halves before spreading with butter. Pack sandwiches in plastic bags and freeze.

Cook 1 sandwich, uncovered, on high 1 minute.

Cook 2 sandwiches, uncovered, on high 1 minute 45 seconds.

BOLOGNA CHEESEWICHES

Some like them hot, some like them cold; take your choice

1 lb. bologna　　　　　　　　**12 hamburger buns, split**
2 medium dill pickles　　　　**Butter or margarine**
½ c. ketchup　　　　　　　　　**12 slices process American**
¼ c. bottled barbecue sauce　　**cheese**

Put bologna and pickles through food chopper. Stir in ketchup and barbecue sauce.

Butter bun halves completely to edges. Spread bottom halves with bologna mixture, lay on cheese slices and cover with bun tops. Wrap individually in aluminum foil, using the drugstore wrap. Freeze.

To heat, place wrapped sandwich in unheated oven. Turn oven to 425° and bake 30 minutes. Or thaw wrapped sandwich in refrigerator and eat cold. Makes 12 sandwiches.

To Use Microwave Oven: Toast bun halves before spreading with butter. Pack sandwiches in plastic bags and freeze.

Cook 1 sandwich, covered with waxed paper, on defrost 2 minutes. Uncover and cook on high 45 seconds.

Cook 2 sandwiches, covered with waxed paper, on defrost 3 minutes. Uncover and cook on high 1½ minutes.

OVEN-FREEZER MEATBALLS

With meatballs and hard rolls in freezer, and barbecue or spaghetti sauce on hand, it's easy to make sandwiches

3 eggs	**⅔ c. finely chopped onion**
½ c. milk	**3 tsp. salt**
4 slices bread, torn in	**¼ tsp. pepper**
bite-size pieces	**3 lbs. ground beef**

Beat eggs in large mixing bowl. Stir in milk, bread, onion, salt and pepper. Add beef, mixing well. Form into 72 (1″) balls. Bake in 2 (15×10×1″) jelly roll pans in 375° oven 25 to 30 minutes. Remove meatballs to another pan. Cool. Place in freezer just until frozen. Package in plastic freezer bags and return to freezer. Makes 6 dozen.

BARBECUED MEATBALL SANDWICH

4 Oven-Freezer Meatballs, frozen

2 tblsp. bottled barbecue sauce

1 tblsp. tomato juice or water

1 hard roll, split

Place frozen meatballs, barbecue sauce and tomato juice in small saucepan. Bring to a boil. Reduce heat, cover and simmer 7 minutes. Serve in hard roll. Makes 1 sandwich.

To make 6 sandwiches: Use 24 meatballs, 1 c. barbecue sauce, 2 tblsp. tomato juice or water. Simmer 8 to 10 minutes.

To Use Microwave Oven: For 1 sandwich, place 4 frozen meatballs in 10 oz. glass casserole. Top with 2 tblsp. bottled barbecue sauce. Cover and cook on high 1½ minutes. Serve in hard roll.

For 2 sandwiches, place 4 meatballs in each of 2 (10 oz.) glass casseroles. Top each with 2 tblsp. bottled barbecue sauce. Cover and cook on high 2½ minutes.

ITALIAN MEATBALL SANDWICH

4 Oven-Freezer Meatballs, frozen

¼ c. spaghetti sauce

1 hard roll, split

Grated Parmesan cheese (optional)

Place frozen meatballs and sauce in small saucepan. Bring to a boil. Reduce heat, cover and simmer 7 minutes. Stir occasionally. Sprinkle with Parmesan cheese. Serve in hard roll. Makes 1 sandwich.

To make 6 sandwiches: Use 24 meatballs and 1¼ c. spaghetti sauce. Cook 8 to 10 minutes. Serve in hard rolls, split.

To Use Microwave Oven: For 1 sandwich, place 4 frozen meat-balls in 10 oz. glass casserole. Top with 2 tblsp. spaghetti sauce. Cover and cook on high 2 minutes. Sprinkle with Parmesan cheese and serve in hard roll.

For 2 sandwiches, place 4 frozen meatballs in each of 2 (10 oz.) glass casseroles. Top each with 2 tblsp. spaghetti sauce. Cover and cook on high 3½ minutes.

BASIC HAMBURGER PATTIES

When someone misses a meal or wants a hearty snack, broil a quick hamburger. This meat mixture has a pleasing, subtle flavor. Good with Marinated Tomatoes and Onions (see Index)

2 lbs. ground beef	**½ tsp. pepper**
½ c. chopped onion	**½ c. tomato juice**
1½ tsp. seasoned salt	

Combine all ingredients. Form into 8 patties. Wrap individually with plastic wrap and freeze. When frozen, store in plastic bag.

To serve, broil or panbroil as many patties as you want, still frozen or thawed. Serve in hamburger buns. Makes 8 servings.

PIZZA MUFFINS

Prepare these and keep in freezer ready to heat as needed

6 English muffins, split	**1 (8 oz.) can pizza sauce**
Butter or margarine	**6 oz. shredded mozzarella**
½ lb. pizza sausage	**cheese (1½ c.)**

Butter muffin halves completely to edges. Brown sausage; drain off excess fat. Spread muffins with pizza sauce; sprinkle with sausage and cheese. Place on baking sheet and freeze. When frozen, store in plastic bag in freezer. Makes 12 servings.

To serve, heat frozen unwrapped muffin in 475° oven for 12 to 15 minutes.

To Use Microwave Oven: Heat 1 frozen pizza muffin, uncovered, on high 1½ minutes.

Heat 2 frozen pizzas, uncovered, on high 3 minutes.

SWISS SALMON SANDWICHES

Fix and refrigerate sandwiches when you know members of the family will eat at different times. Do not freeze these

1 (8 oz.) can salmon, drained and flaked	2 tblsp. sliced stuffed green olives
4 oz. shredded Swiss cheese (1 c.)	¼ c. mayonnaise or salad dressing
2 tblsp. chopped dill pickle	1 tblsp. lemon juice
2 tblsp. chopped onion	6 hamburger buns, split

Combine salmon, cheese, pickle, onion, olives, mayonnaise and lemon juice. Spread between buns. Wrap individually in aluminum foil. Chill. When ready to eat, place wrapped sandwich in unheated oven. Turn oven to 400° and bake 20 minutes. Makes 6 sandwiches.

To Use Microwave Oven: Toast bun halves before assembling sandwich. Cook 1 sandwich, uncovered, on high 45 seconds.

Cook 2 sandwiches, uncovered, on high 1½ minutes.

ITALIAN-STYLE SLOPPY JOES

A quick, easy and tasty way to use leftover pot roast

1 lb. leftover pot roast, cubed	1 beef bouillon cube
1 (8 oz.) can pizza sauce	9 hamburger buns, split
¼ c. water	Grated Parmesan cheese

Combine beef, pizza sauce, water and bouillon cube in skillet. Simmer, covered, 10 minutes. Serve between split buns, sprinkling meat with Parmesan cheese. Makes 3 cups meat mixture or 9 servings.

TUNA BUTTER

Spread on crisp whole wheat crackers, celery or toast

½ c. butter or margarine
1 (7 oz.) can water-pack
  tuna, drained and flaked
⅓ c. mayonnaise or salad
  dressing

2 tblsp. lemon juice
2 tblsp. chopped
  pimiento-stuffed olives

Cream butter until fluffy. Beat in tuna, mayonnaise and lemon juice. Stir in chopped olives. Store in refrigerator. Serve with raw vegetable dippers and crackers. Makes 1¾ cups.

SCANDINAVIAN EGG SALAD

Nothing bland about this egg salad. Men like it on rye bread

8 hard-cooked eggs,
  chopped
1½ c. chopped celery
½ c. chopped dill pickle
¼ c. chopped onion
¼ c. drained capers
1 (2 oz.) can anchovy fillets,
  drained and chopped

½ c. mayonnaise or salad
  dressing
¼ tsp. dried dill weed
¼ tsp. salt
⅛ tsp. pepper

Combine all ingredients. Cover and chill. Use within 2 days. Serve on rye bread or toast. Makes 1 quart.

BRAN MEAT LOAF

Loaf cuts neatly. Use leftover slices for sandwich snacks

2 eggs	1 tblsp. Worcestershire
½ c. whole bran cereal	sauce
⅓ c. cracker crumbs	2 tsp. salt
¼ c. nonfat dry milk	¼ tsp. pepper
1 (8 oz.) can tomato sauce	¼ tsp. rubbed sage
½ c. finely chopped onion	2 lbs. ground beef

Beat eggs in large mixing bowl. Thoroughly mix in remaining ingredients. Form into 10×5″ loaf in 13×9×2″ baking pan. Bake in 350° oven 1 hour and 15 minutes. Makes 10 main-dish servings.

BRAUNSCHWEIGER DIP

Liver is such a good source of iron, even a little bit counts. Serve in bowl with raw vegetable dippers and assorted rye and whole wheat crackers

½ lb. braunschweiger	1 tblsp. ketchup
1 c. dairy sour cream	1 tsp. Worcestershire sauce
2 tblsp. dry onion soup mix	Few drops Tabasco sauce

With fork mix together braunschweiger and sour cream. Add remaining ingredients and beat thoroughly. Cover and chill at least 1 hour. Makes about 2 cups.

SLOPPY JOE BARBECUE SANDWICHES

If you fix these sandwiches for family lunch or supper, you can be sure the teen-agers will demolish any leftovers. It's a favorite snack after the game

2 lbs. ground beef
1 c. chopped onion
1 c. chopped celery
2 tblsp. brown sugar, firmly
    packed
2 tsp. salt
½ tsp. dry mustard
¼ tsp. pepper

1 (14 oz.) bottle ketchup
    (1 c.)
¾ c. water
¼ c. vinegar
2 tblsp. Worcestershire
    sauce
12 hamburger buns, split

Brown beef in large skillet. Pour off excess fat. Add remaining ingredients except buns. Simmer covered, 15 minutes. Uncover and simmer 5 minutes. Serve hot between split buns. Cool leftover meat mixture, cover and store in refrigerator. Will keep up to 3 days. Reheat to serve. Makes 12 servings.

TUNA COCKTAIL FOR SANDWICHES

Beautifully seasoned sauce makes a new kind of tuna sandwich

2 (7 oz.) cans tuna, drained
½ c. chopped celery
2 tblsp. chopped green
    onion
½ c. chili sauce

2 tblsp. lemon juice
1 tblsp. horseradish
Few drops Tabasco sauce
¼ tsp. salt

Combine all ingredients. Cover and chill at least 1 hour. Spread on toasted slices of French or whole wheat bread. Makes 2½ cups.

EASY DENVER SANDWICH

Quick, dependable, old-time sandwich has a new ingredient, bacon-flavored vegetable protein chips. If you have the seasoning in your cupboard, by all means use it in this snack

1 tblsp. chopped green pepper	2 tsp. bacon-flavored vegetable protein chips (optional)
1 tsp. butter or margarine, melted	1 tsp. instant onion
1 egg	Dash of salt
1 tblsp. milk	Dash of pepper

In small skillet cook green pepper in butter until soft.

Beat egg; stir in remaining ingredients. Pour into skillet. Cook over low heat. As mixture begins to set at bottom and sides, gently lift cooked portions with spatula so thin, uncooked portion can flow to bottom. Cook until thickened throughout but still moist. Serve in bun or between slices of buttered toast or bread. Makes 1 sandwich.

BURGER DOGS

Crackers provide a faint, pleasant bacon flavor, but you can substitute other flavors. Wrapping each burger individually will reduce the reheating time

2 eggs	¼ c. grated onion
¾ c. milk	1½ tsp. salt
1 c. crushed bacon flavor crackers	⅛ tsp. pepper
	2 lbs. ground beef

Beat eggs in large bowl. Stir in remaining ingredients. Divide into 12 equal sized balls. Shape like frankfurters, 5″ long; place on broiler pan. Broil 3″ from heat in preheated broiler until lightly browned, about 5 minutes. Turn and broil 4 minutes more. Cool. Wrap individually in aluminum foil, using the drug-store wrap. Freeze.

To heat, place frozen, wrapped, burger dogs in 400° oven and bake 25 minutes or until hot. Serve in hot dog buns. Makes 12 servings.

To Use Microwave Oven: Freeze burger dogs without wrapping. When frozen, place in plastic bag and return to freezer.

Cook 1 burger dog, uncovered, 2 minutes on high.

Cook 2 burger dogs, uncovered, 3 minutes on high. Serve in hot dog buns.

STUFFED FRANKFURTERS

You can stuff frankfurters up to twelve hours before serving. Keep in refrigerator. Or freeze them up to a week before using. Bake them; add cheese just before serving

½ c. chopped onions	½ c. water
¼ c. butter or margarine	¼ c. ketchup
1 (8 oz.) pkg. corn bread stuffing mix (3 c.)	2 (1 lb.) pkgs. large frankfurters (10 to 12)
1 (8 oz.) can pork and beans with tomato sauce	6 slices sharp process American cheese

Cook onion in butter until soft. Combine with stuffing mix, undrained pork and beans, water and ketchup. Cut frankfurters lengthwise, but not quite through. Spread open. Mound stuffing on top frankfurters. Cover and refrigerate, or freeze to bake later. To freeze, wrap frankfurters individually in foil or place in covered pan. Store in freezer up to 1 week.

To heat refrigerated frankfurters, place in 400° oven for 10 to 15 minutes. Place ½ cheese slice on each frankfurter. Return to oven until cheese is melted, 2 to 3 minutes.

To heat frozen frankfurters, unwrap and bake in 400° oven 20 minutes. Top with ½ cheese slice and return to oven until cheese melts, 2 to 3 minutes. Makes 10 to 12 servings.

To Use Microwave Oven: Cook 1 refrigerated stuffed frankfurter topped with ½ cheese slice, uncovered, on high 1 minute.

Cook 2 refrigerated stuffed frankfurters topped with cheese, uncovered, on high 1½ minutes.

Cook 1 frozen stuffed frankfurter, uncovered, on defrost 4 minutes. Top with ½ cheese slice. Cook on high 1 minute.

Cook 2 frozen stuffed frankfurters, uncovered, on defrost 5 minutes. Top each with ½ cheese slice. Cook on high 1½ minutes.

TUNA CHEESE BUNS

Frozen sandwiches come in handy for snacks and for the family lunch or supper on a busy day. Serve piping hot

1 (7 oz.) can tuna, drained and flaked	⅓ c. dairy sour cream
	3 tblsp. pickle relish
6 oz. shredded sharp process American cheese (1½ c.)	8 hamburger buns, split
	Butter or margarine

Combine tuna, cheese, sour cream and relish. Butter bun halves completely to edges. Fill with tuna mixture. Wrap sandwiches individually in aluminum foil, using the drugstore wrap. Freeze.

To serve, place frozen, wrapped sandwich in unheated oven. Turn heat to 400° and bake 25 to 30 minutes. Makes 8 sandwiches.

To Use Microwave Oven: Toast buns before spreading with butter and tuna mixture. Freeze without wrapping. When frozen, place in plastic bag. To serve cook 1 frozen sandwich, covered with paper toweling, on defrost 2 minutes. Uncover and cook on high 30 seconds.

Cook 2 frozen sandwiches, covered with paper toweling, on defrost 3 minutes. Uncover and cook on high 1 minute.

TACOS

Tacos, or Mexican sandwiches, have gained wide popularity North of the Border. Many supermarkets now carry taco shells ready for filling with ground beef mixtures

2½ c. Taco Filling (recipe follows)
24 taco shells
6 oz. shredded Cheddar cheese (1½ c.)

Shredded lettuce
Quartered cherry tomatoes or chopped tomato
Bottled taco sauce (optional)

Heat filling. Place about 2 tblsp. of it in each taco shell. Sprinkle with about 1 tblsp. shredded cheese and a little chopped lettuce. Add tomatoes for garnish. Sprinkle with taco sauce, if desired.

TACO FILLING

1 lb. ground beef
1 c. chopped onion
1 tsp. salt
1 tsp. chili powder
½ tsp. ground cumin

½ tsp. crushed red peppers (optional)
½ tsp. instant minced garlic
¼ tsp. dried oregano
1 (8 oz.) can tomato sauce

In skillet, cook ground beef and onion until beef is browned. Drain off excess fat. Add remaining ingredients and simmer, uncovered, 10 minutes. Stir occasionally. Mixture may be cooled and refrigerated up to 3 days. Makes 2½ cups, enough to fill 24 taco shells.

INDIVIDUAL PIZZA CRUSTS

Bake, fill and freeze ready for speedy heating and eating

1 pkg. active dry yeast	1¼ c. warm water (110 to
3½ to 4 c. all-purpose flour	115°)
½ tsp. salt	Vegetable oil

In large mixer bowl combine yeast, 1¼ c. flour and salt. Add warm water and beat at low speed ½ minute, scraping sides of bowl constantly. Beat 3 minutes at high speed, scraping sides of bowl occasionally.

By hand, stir in enough remaining flour to make a moderately stiff dough. Turn out on lightly floured surface and knead until smooth and elastic, 8 to 10 minutes.

Place in greased bowl, turning dough to grease all sides. Cover and let rise in warm place until double, about 45 minutes.

Punch down. Divide dough into 8 balls. Roll each ball to make a 5″ round and place on greased baking sheet. Gently stretch rounds to 6″ diameter, building up edges slightly. Prick with fork as for pie shell. Brush lightly with oil.

Bake in 425° oven 5 minutes. Remove and let cool on baking sheets. Freeze unfilled, if desired. Makes 8 crusts.

HOMEMADE PIZZA SAUCE

Flavor is what counts in a sauce and this one really has it

1 (15 oz.) can tomato sauce	½ tsp. dried oregano,
½ c. finely chopped onion	crushed
1 clove garlic, minced	½ tsp. dried basil, crushed
1 tblsp. dried parsley flakes	

In saucepan, combine tomato sauce, onion, garlic, parsley, oregano and basil. Simmer, uncovered, 15 minutes, stirring occasionally. Makes 1½ cups.

SAUSAGE PIZZAS

Italian flavor earns for these pizzas a loyal following

½ lb. pizza sausage
1½ c. Homemade Pizza
   Sauce
8 Individual Pizza Crusts

4 oz. shredded mozzarella
   cheese (1 c.)
½ c. grated Parmesan
   cheese

Brown pizza sausage in skillet; drain off excess fat.

Spread Homemade Pizza Sauce on cooled crusts; sprinkle evenly with sausage and cheeses. Freeze on baking sheets. When frozen, store in plastic bags. Makes 8 pizzas.

To serve, place frozen pizzas directly on rack in 475° oven and bake 10 to 12 minutes or until nicely browned.

HAMBURGER PIZZAS

A welcome change from ground beef served in buns

½ lb. ground beef
½ tsp. salt
⅛ tsp. pepper
1½ c. Homademade Pizza
   Sauce
8 Individual Pizza Crusts

½ c. chopped green pepper
4 oz. shredded mozzarella
   cheese (1 c.)
½ c. grated Parmesan
   cheese

Brown ground beef in skillet; drain off excess fat. Stir in salt and pepper.

Spread pizza sauce on cooled crusts; sprinkle evenly with

ground beef, green pepper and cheeses. Freeze on baking sheet. When frozen, place in plastic bag and store in freezer.

To serve, place frozen pizzas directly on rack in 475° oven and bake 10 to 12 minutes or until nicely browned. Makes 8 servings.

Don't overlook the substantial sandwiches in Chapter 5 featuring milk products. They are Cheesy Fishburgers, Mexican Cheeseburgers and Cottage Cheese Sandwiches. Consult Index for page numbers.

SUBSTANTIAL SOUPS

CHICKEN VEGETABLE SOUP

Make this hearty soup for the family but save out a few individual servings to freeze and reheat later for snacks

1 (3 lb.) broiler-fryer chicken, cut up	2½ tsp. salt
6 c. water	¼ tsp. pepper
⅓ c. chopped celery	1 c. sliced carrots
⅓ c. chopped onion	1½ c. fine noodles
	½ c. frozen peas

In Dutch oven combine chicken, water, celery, onion, salt and pepper. Bring to a boil. Reduce heat and simmer, covered, until chicken is tender, about 50 minutes. Remove chicken from broth. Cut in small pieces, discarding skin and bones.

Return chicken to broth. Add carrots and bring to a boil. Reduce heat and simmer, covered, 10 minutes. Add noodles and peas; continue cooking 5 minutes.

Remove portion of soup to freeze for snacks. Cook remaining

soup until carrots and noodles are tender, about 10 minutes. Makes in all about 2 quarts.

Soup for Snacks: Ladle ¾ c. soup into 1-cup freezer containers, cool, cover and freeze. To reheat, place container in pan of warm water to loosen soup; turn soup into small saucepan. Cover and simmer until heated through.

To Use Microwave Oven: Ladle ¾ c. soup into half-pint glass jars or 10 oz. glass casseroles; cover and freeze. To reheat, remove metal lid, cover unthawed soup with waxed paper or glass casserole lid and place in microwave oven.

Cook 1 serving on high 4 minutes. Stir; cook 1 minute more. Let stand 2 minutes.

Cook 2 servings on high 6 minutes. Stir; cook 1 minute more. Let stand 2 minutes.

ITALIAN VEGETABLE SOUP

Using undrained beans conserves nutrients usually poured down the drain. Sprinkle piping hot soup generously with grated Parmesan cheese and serve with French or Italian bread

1½ lb. stewing beef, cut in 1″ cubes	¼ tsp. pepper
2 tblsp. vegetable oil	1 c. chopped onion
5 c. water	1 c. chopped celery
5 beef bouillon cubes	1 (16 oz.) can green beans
1 (16 oz.) can tomatoes, cut up	1 (15 oz.) can kidney beans
2 tsp. salt	1½ c. sliced carrots
1½ tsp. mixed Italian seasonings	¾ c. shell macaroni
	Grated Parmesan cheese

In Dutch oven brown beef in oil. Add water, bouillon cubes, tomatoes, seasonings, onions and celery. Bring to a boil. Reduce heat and simmer, covered, about 1½ hours, or until meat is tender. Add undrained beans and carrots. Bring to a boil. Reduce heat and simmer, covered, 10 minutes. Add macaroni. Continue simmering 7 minutes.

Remove portion of soup to freeze for snacks. Continue simmering remaining soup until carrots and macaroni are tender, about 15 minutes. Makes in all about 3½ quarts.

Soup for Snacks: Ladle ¾ c. soup into 1-cup freezer containers, cool, cover and freeze. To reheat, place container in pan of warm water to loosen soup; turn soup into small saucepan. Cover and simmer until heated through.

To Use Microwave Oven: Ladle ¾ c. soup into half-pint glass jars or 10 oz. glass casseroles; cover and freeze. To reheat, remove metal lid, cover unthawed soup with waxed paper or glass casserole lid and place in microwave oven.

Cook 1 serving on high 4 minutes. Stir; cook 1 minute more. Let stand 2 minutes.

Cook 2 servings on high 6 minutes. Stir; cook 1 minute more. Let stand 2 minutes.

TEXAS VEGETABLE SOUP

People who like chili praise this hamburger soup

1 lb. ground beef	1 (15 oz.) can kidney beans
1 c. chopped onion	1 c. sliced carrots
¾ c. chopped celery	1 garlic clove, minced
5 c. water	6 beef bouillon cubes
1 (28 oz.) can tomatoes, cut up	2 tsp. salt
1 (16 oz.) can whole kernel corn	1½ tsp. chili powder
	¼ tsp. pepper

In Dutch oven cook beef, onion and celery until beef is browned. Drain off excess fat. Add remaining ingredients. Bring to a boil. Reduce heat and simmer, covered, 10 minutes.

Remove portion of soup to freeze for snacks. Cook remaining soup until carrots are tender, about 15 minutes. Makes in all 3¾ quarts.

Soup for Snacks: Ladle ¾ c. soup into 1-cup freezer containers, cool, cover and freeze. To reheat, place container in pan of warm water to loosen soup; turn soup into small saucepan. Cover and simmer until heated through.

To Use Microwave Oven: Ladle ¾ c. soup into half-pint glass jars or 10 oz. glass casseroles; cover and freeze. To reheat, remove metal lid, cover unthawed soup with waxed paper or glass casserole lid and place in microwave oven.

Cook 1 serving on high 4 minutes. Stir; cook 1 minute more. Let stand 2 minutes.

Cook 2 servings on high 6 minutes. Stir; cook 1 minute more. Let stand 2 minutes.

NOURISHING MINIATURE CASSEROLES

SNACKERS' CASSEROLES

Individual casseroles are ideal for households where people eat at different hours. Your odd-hour eaters will like the mild hickory smoke flavor in this recipe

1 lb. ground beef	2 c. milk
¾ c. chopped onion	1 (6 oz.) roll process cheese
1½ tsp. salt	food, hickory smoke flavor
¼ tsp. pepper	4 c. peeled, cooked, cubed
¼ tsp. dried thyme	potatoes (4 to 5 medium)
¼ c. butter or margarine	¼ c. cornflake crumbs
¼ c. flour	

In skillet cook ground beef and onion until beef is browned. Pour off excess fat. Stir in 1 tsp. salt, pepper and thyme.

In saucepan melt butter; stir in flour and remaining ½ tsp. salt. Add milk. Cook, stirring, until mixture boils and thickens. Add cheese food, stirring until melted. Remove from heat and stir in ground beef mixture and potatoes.

Spoon into 7 (5×1¼″) aluminum foil tart pans. Sprinkle cornflake crumbs on top. Cover each with plastic wrap and refrigerate up to 2 days. Do not freeze.

To serve, uncover and bake in 350° oven 30 to 40 minutes, or until bubbly. Makes 7 servings.

To Use Microwave Oven: Place ¾ c. beef mixture in each of 7 (10 oz.) glass casseroles. Cover and refrigerate.

Cook 1 casserole, covered, 2 minutes on high. Let stand 1 minute before serving.

Cook 2 casseroles, covered, 4½ minutes on high. Let stand 2 minutes before serving.

GROUND BEEF MINI-MEAL

Miniature casserole is just right for anyone eating alone

1 lb. ground beef	⅛ tsp. pepper
1 c. chopped onion	1 (16 oz.) can green beans,
½ c. chopped green pepper	drained
1 (15 oz.) can tomato sauce	1 (15 oz.) can kidney beans,
½ c. water	drained and rinsed
4 oz. noodles	1 (12 oz.) can whole kernel
1½ tsp. salt	corn, drained
¼ tsp. chili powder	

In skillet cook ground beef, onion and green pepper until beef is browned. Drain off excess fat. Add tomato sauce, water, noodles, salt, chili powder and pepper. Bring to a boil. Reduce heat and simmer, covered, 5 minutes. Stir in remaining ingredients.

Spoon into 10 (5×1¼") foil tart pans. Cool and freeze. Wrap in foil and return to freezer.

To serve, place frozen wrapped casserole(s) in 450° oven and bake 40 minutes. Makes 10 servings.

To Use Microwave Oven: Put ¾ c. beef-vegetable mixture into each of 10 (10 oz.) casseroles. Cool, cover and freeze.

Cook 1 casserole, covered, on high 4 minutes. Stir; cook 1½ minutes more. Let stand 2 minutes.

Cook 2 casseroles, covered, on high 5 minutes. Stir; cook 2 minutes more. Let stand 2 minutes.

TUNA-VEGETABLE CASSEROLE

First choice frozen casserole in family with two lone eaters

2 (10¾ oz.) cans condensed
  cream of mushroom soup
⅔ c. milk
1 tsp. instant minced onion
½ tsp. salt
⅛ tsp. pepper

2 (7 oz.) cans tuna, drained
  and flaked
4 oz. narrow noodles
2 (10 oz.) pkgs. frozen
  mixed vegetables

In large mixing bowl blend together soup and milk. Stir in onion, salt, pepper and tuna.

Cook noodles in 1 qt. boiling, salted water 5 minutes. Drain and stir into tuna mixture.

In saucepan bring 1½ c. salted water to boiling. Add frozen vegetables, return to a boil, cover and cook 1 minute. Separate vegetables with a fork. Continue cooking 6 minutes; drain. Add to tuna mixture.

Place ¾ c. mixture in each of 10 (5×1½") aluminum foil

tart pans. Cool and freeze. Wrap in foil and return to freezer. To serve, place frozen, wrapped casserole(s) in 450° oven and bake 30 minutes. Makes 10 servings.

To Use Microwave Oven: Place ¾ c. tuna mixture in each of 10 (10 oz.) glass casseroles. Cool, cover and freeze.

Cook 1 casserole, covered, on high 4 minutes. Stir; cook 1½ minutes more. Let stand 2 minutes.

Cook 2 casseroles, covered, on high 6 minutes. Stir; cook 2 minutes more. Let stand 2 minutes.

INDIVIDUAL CHICKEN CASSEROLES

Heat this substantial snack from freezer for the member of the family who missed a meal. Chicken, vegetables and spaghetti give it main dish status and good food value

1 (2½ to 3 lb.) broiler-fryer chicken, cut up	½ c. chopped onion
3 c. water	2 tsp. salt
1 small onion, sliced	½ tsp. dried oregano
1 (6″) celery branch	¼ tsp. pepper
1 tsp. salt	1 (7 oz.) box bite-size spaghetti
4 peppercorns	1 (16 oz.) can peas, drained
1 (15 oz.) can tomato sauce	Grated Parmesan cheese
1½ c. sliced carrots	

Place chicken, 3 c. water, sliced onion, celery, 1 tsp. salt and peppercorns in Dutch oven. Bring to a boil. Reduce heat and simmer, covered, 50 minutes or until chicken is tender. Drain, reserving broth. Strain broth. Cut chicken in small pieces, discarding bones and skin.

Combine broth and tomato sauce in Dutch oven. Bring to a boil. Add carrots, chopped onion, 2 tsp. salt, oregano and pepper. Return to a boil, boil 3 minutes, and add spaghetti. Bring to a boil again and boil 3 more minutes, stirring occasionally. Remove from heat. Add chicken and peas. Spoon into 10 or 11 (5×1¼″) aluminum foil tart pans. Cool and freeze. Wrap in foil and return to freezer.

To serve, place frozen, wrapped casserole in 450° oven and bake 45 minutes. Unwrap and sprinkle with Parmesan cheese. Makes 10 or 11 servings.

To Use Microwave Oven: Place ¾ c. chicken-spaghetti mixture into each of 10 or 11 (10 oz.) glass casseroles. Cool, cover and freeze.

Cook 1 casserole, covered, on high 4 minutes. Stir; cook 1½ minutes more. Let stand 2 minutes.

Cook 2 casseroles, covered, on high 6 minutes. Stir; cook 2 minutes more. Let stand 2 minutes.

Chapter 7

SWEETS TO EAT WITH
A BETTER CONSCIENCE

To tune desserts into today's diet, step up their nutritive merits. You cannot wave a wand and eliminate the appeal of sweet, rich desserts—most people like them too much! But you can introduce changes. Try our adaptations of some of the family favorites. By adding or changing ingredients, these recipes enable you, with good conscience, to offer sweets to your family.

Cooking with smaller amounts of sugar and fat needn't subtract from the happiness eating desserts affords. Such desserts will be less sweet and rich than those your mother made, but they taste mighty good. And what is of major importance, our knowledge of nutrition is greater than it used to be and the dessert-type recipes we've worked out for this book contain extra nutrients that contribute to good health. Not one of these desserts contains calories without nutrients.

The size of dessert servings also can be handled judiciously—for overweight family members, for instance. Fast-growing teenagers and physically active men and women may eat larger pieces of cake and more cookies without crowding other nutritive foods from their diets.

A pie divided in eight wedges tastes as delicious as when cut in six. You can slice a cake in big, medium or little pieces. Few people will pay attention to the size if presented without comment or fanfare. And you will find just a touch of sweetness frequently satisfies.

Cookies are the favorite dessert-type snack. You can load them with health-promoting ingredients, and serve only the number your family needs. Our Sunflower Refrigerator Cookies are a splendid example. Among the contents of these crisp cookies are whole wheat flour, wheat germ, rolled oats and sunflower seeds.

Boys in our test families frequently singled out Super Chocolate Chip Cookies. In addition to chocolate pieces, they contain peanuts, sunflower seeds, whole wheat flour and wheat germ.

Pea-nutty Cookies never fail to extract compliments. Peanuts are native American and like other legumes, they supply protein, B-vitamins, iron and other minerals. They are kind to food budgets, especially in years when the harvest is bountiful. Many of the recipes in this book owe their improved nutritional properties in part to peanuts and peanut butter.

Skip the dessert in lunch and/or dinner when you plan to serve a dessert snack between meals. That is a good way to cut down on sugar and fat. For example, when you've invited friends to come by after dinner, postpone your own meal ending until later, when you can enjoy it with your guests. Waiting a few hours usually is acceptable—it can become a family habit.

A slice of homemade cake with a cup of tea or coffee, or a glass of milk or fruit juice, make a pleasing refreshment. Among the recipes that follow for nutritionally up-dated cakes are regal Orange Sponge and country style Applesauce Cakes. Both contain protein-rich soy flour, available in many supermarkets. Orange-flavored Cranberry Calico Cake, a beauty for the holiday season and other special occasions, is another excellent cake that tempts the eye.

Omit frostings to cut down on sweets—dust cake lightly with confectioners sugar instead. If your family is not easily weaned from the traditional toppings, spread them thin. Serve thin glazes—without comment.

Pies occasionally deserve a place in between-meal eating. Promote one-crust pies by serving them—also without a sales talk. Be sure the filling is primed with nutrients. Sweet Potato Pecan and Pioneer Apricot Prune Pies are praiseworthy examples. The yellow-orange color of sweet potatoes and dried apricots promise the dessert will deliver Vitamin A.

Specialize in what some women refer to as milk-and-egg desserts. Swedish Apple Pudding with Custard Sauce is one homespun example. Maple Custards, made with nonfat milk, and High-Hat Banana Custards are other specials.

Use the recipes in this chapter to help improve the nutritional quality of dessert-snacks and to provide treats tuned to today.

SNACK COOKIES

SUNFLOWER REFRIGERATOR COOKIES

These cookies are crisp, thin and flavorful, a whole grain snack

½ c. butter or margarine
½ c. sugar
½ c. brown sugar, firmly
  packed
1 egg
1 tsp. vanilla
1½ c. quick-cooking rolled
  oats

¾ c. stirred whole wheat
  flour
¼ c. wheat germ
½ tsp. baking soda
¼ tsp. salt
¾ c. dry-roasted sunflower
  seeds

Cream together butter and sugars. Add egg and vanilla; beat thoroughly.

Stir together rolled oats, whole wheat flour, wheat germ, soda and salt. Stir into creamed mixture. Stir in sunflower seeds.

Divide dough in half and form in two rolls about 2" in diameter. Wrap tightly in waxed paper and chill at least 4 hours. Cut in ¼" slices and place 2" apart on ungreased baking sheet.

Bake in 375° oven 10 to 12 minutes or until lightly browned. Cool on racks. Makes about 4 dozen.

PEA-NUTTY COOKIES

Peanut butter is part of the shortening in these crisp, delicious cookies. Together with chopped peanuts, it contributes protein, several B-vitamins and important minerals

½ c. peanut butter
½ c. butter or margarine
½ c. sugar
½ c. brown sugar, firmly
   packed
1 egg
1 tsp. vanilla

1¼ c. sifted all-purpose
   flour
¾ tsp. baking soda
½ tsp. baking powder
¼ tsp. salt
1 c. finely chopped peanuts

Cream together peanut butter and butter. Add sugars and beat until light and fluffy. Add egg and vanilla; beat thoroughly.

Sift together flour, baking soda, baking powder and salt. Stir into creamed mixture. Cover and chill at least 1 hour.

Roll heaping teaspoonfuls of dough in balls. Roll in chopped peanuts. Place 3" apart on greased baking sheet. Flatten balls with bottom of drinking glass.

Bake in 375° oven 10 to 12 minutes, or until lightly browned. Cool on racks. Makes about 3 dozen.

SUPER CHOCOLATE CHIP COOKIES

These whole grain "health cookies" really taste good

½ c. butter or margarine
½ c. brown sugar, firmly
  packed
1 egg
½ tsp. vanilla
½ c. stirred whole wheat
  flour
½ c. wheat germ

2 tblsp. nonfat dry milk
½ tsp. baking soda
1 (6 oz.) pkg. semisweet
  chocolate pieces
½ c. dry-roasted sunflower
  seeds
½ c. chopped peanuts

Cream together butter and sugar. Add egg and vanilla; beat until light and fluffy.

Stir together whole wheat flour, wheat germ, dry milk and soda. Stir into creamed mixture. Stir in chocolate pieces, sunflower seeds and peanuts. Drop by rounded teaspoonfuls 2″ apart on greased baking sheet.

Bake in 350° oven 10 to 12 minutes or until lightly browned. Cool on racks. Makes 3 dozen.

HONEYED RAISIN COOKIES

Rolling unbaked cookie balls in wheat germ speckles them attractively. Honey, lemon peel and raisins do something especially good to the flavor of these country-type cookies

½ c. butter or margarine
½ c. sugar
½ c. honey
1 tsp. grated lemon peel
1 egg
2 c. sifted all-purpose flour

1 tsp. baking powder
¼ tsp. salt
½ c. wheat germ
1 c. raisins
⅓ c. wheat germ

Cream butter; add sugar and honey and beat until light and fluffy. Add lemon peel and egg, beating thoroughly.

Sift together flour, baking powder and salt; stir into creamed mixture. Stir in ½ c. wheat germ and raisins. Cover and chill at least 1 hour.

Shape dough into 1″ balls; roll in remaining ⅓ c. wheat germ. Place 2″ apart on greased baking sheet. Flatten slightly with fingers. Bake in 400° oven 8 to 10 minutes or until lightly browned. Cool on racks. Makes about 3 dozen.

CASHEW-DATE DROPS

If you like the taste of cashews, the kidney-shaped fruit of a South American tree, you will enjoy these cookies. While not botanically a nut, cashews have the same nutrients as nuts—considerable fat, protein, B-vitamins and minerals. Serve with a glass of milk or a hot beverage

½ c. butter or margarine
½ c. brown sugar, firmly
   packed
¼ c. honey
1 egg
1 tsp. vanilla

1½ c. all-purpose flour
½ tsp. baking powder
½ tsp. salt
1 c. chopped dates
1 (7 oz.) jar cashew nuts,
   chopped (1⅓ c.)

Cream together butter and brown sugar until light and fluffy. Add honey, egg and vanilla, beating until well blended.

Sift together flour, baking powder and salt. Stir into creamed mixture. Stir in dates. Cover and chill at least 1 hour.

Drop by heaping teaspoonfuls into chopped cashews. Roll lightly to coat. Place on greased baking sheet. With bottom of drinking glass, flatten cookies ½″ thick.

Bake in 400° oven 9 to 11 minutes or until lightly browned. Cool on racks. Makes about 3 dozen.

BANANA COOKIES

These cookies are tender, moist, cakelike and good with milk

2½ c. sifted all-purpose
    flour
1 c. sugar
¼ c. stirred soy flour
1½ tsp. baking soda
½ tsp. salt
¼ tsp. ground cinnamon

½ c. butter or margarine
1 c. mashed bananas (about
    2 large)
½ c. buttermilk
2 eggs
1 tsp. vanilla
1 c. chopped nuts

In large mixer bowl combine all ingredients except nuts. Beat at low speed 3 minutes, scraping sides of bowl occasionally. By hand, stir in nuts. Drop by heaping teaspoonfuls 2″ apart on greased baking sheet.

Bake in 375° oven 9 to 11 minutes or until lightly browned. Remove to wire rack with pancake turner. Makes 5½ dozen.

GRANOLA COOKIES

Granola puts the crunchiness and the nutrients of whole grains into these cookies; texture holds up in baking

1¾ c. packaged regular
    granola
1½ c. sifted all-purpose
    flour
¾ c. sugar
¾ c. brown sugar, firmly
    packed
½ c. butter or margarine
½ c. shortening

1 tsp. salt
1 tsp. baking soda
½ tsp. ground cinnamon
1 tsp. vanilla
1 egg
1 c. raisins
¾ c. coarsely chopped
    peanuts

In large mixer bowl combine all ingredients except raisins and peanuts. Beat at low speed just until mixed, scraping bowl constantly. Beat at medium speed 2 minutes, scraping sides of bowl occasionally.

By hand stir in raisins and peanuts. Drop by heaping teaspoonfuls 2″ apart on greased baking sheet.

Bake in 375° oven 10 to 12 minutes or until lightly browned. Cool on racks. Makes 5½ dozen.

RAISIN CARROT OATMEAL COOKIES

These tasty everyday cookies contribute iron, vitamin A and some B-vitamins. You can stir them up easily without using an electric mixer and you may want to double the recipe

⅓ c. brown sugar, firmly
   packed
⅓ c. vegetable oil
⅓ c. light molasses
1 egg
1 c. sifted all-purpose flour
¼ c. nonfat dry milk
1 tsp. salt

½ tsp. baking powder
½ tsp. baking soda
½ tsp. ground cinnamon
1½ c. quick-cooking rolled
   oats
1 c. grated carrots
¾ c. raisins

In mixing bowl beat together brown sugar, oil, molasses and egg.

Sift together flour, dry milk, salt, baking powder, baking soda and cinnamon. Stir into oil mixture until blended. Stir in rolled oats, carrots and raisins. Drop by heaping teaspoonfuls on greased baking sheet.

Bake in 375° oven 10 minutes or until lightly browned. Cool on racks. Makes about 2½ dozen.

MOLASSES GINGER COOKIES

These old-fashioned, country kitchen cookies with crackled tops contain a new-fangled ingredient, protein-rich soy flour. The molasses-ginger taste is nostalgically pleasing

½ c. butter or margarine
¼ c. shortening
1 c. sugar
1 egg
⅓ c. light molasses
1 c. unsifted all-purpose
   flour

1 c. stirred soy flour
1 tsp. baking soda
½ tsp. salt
1½ tsp. ground ginger
1 tsp. ground cinnamon
⅓ c. sugar

In large mixer bowl cream together butter and shortening. Add 1 c. sugar and egg and beat until light and fluffy. Beat in molasses.

Stir together flours, baking soda, salt and spices. Stir into creamed mixture. Cover and chill at least 1 hour.

Form dough into 1″ balls. Roll in remaining ⅓ c. sugar. Place 2″ apart on greased baking sheet.

Bake in 375° oven 10 to 12 minutes or until lightly browned. Cool on racks. Makes 4 dozen.

FRUITED BRAN COOKIES

These cookies skip the oven but they add their share of nutrients to the day's food. Dainty tea cookies with lemon-almond accent

2½ c. whole bran cereal
1 (8 oz.) pkg. chopped dates
¾ c. light raisins
¾ c. flaked coconut
¾ c. chopped, toasted
   almonds

1½ tsp. grated lemon peel
1 (14 oz.) can sweetened
   condensed milk
2 tblsp. lemon juice

Combine cereal, fruits, nuts and lemon peel.

Stir together sweetened condensed milk (not evaporated) and lemon juice; combine with bran mixture. On waxed paper form 4 rolls 1½" in diameter; wrap tightly. Chill at least 1 hour. Cut in ½" slices. Makes about 6 dozen.

OATMEAL FRUIT COOKIES

These wholesome cookies endear themselves to mothers on the lookout for good-for-you foods their children will eat with enthusiasm. Orange flavor is delicate

½ c. butter or margarine
½ c. sugar
½ c. brown sugar, firmly
   packed
1 egg
½ tsp. vanilla
1 c. sifted all-purpose flour
¼ c. nonfat dry milk
½ tsp. baking powder
½ tsp. baking soda

¼ tsp. salt
1 tblsp. water
¾ c. quick-cooking
   rolled oats
½ c. chopped dates
½ c. raisins
½ c. chopped nuts
½ c. flaked coconut
1½ tsp. grated orange peel

Cream butter, beat in sugars and continue beating until mixture is light and fluffy. Beat in egg and vanilla.

Sift together flour, dry milk, baking powder, baking soda and salt. Stir into creamed mixture. Blend in water; stir in remaining ingredients. Form level tablespoonfuls of mixture into balls. Place 2″ apart on greased baking sheet.

Bake in 375° oven 10 to 12 minutes or until lightly browned. Cool on racks. Makes 3 dozen.

GOOD HEALTH BARS

These cookies deserve their name. And everyone likes the taste

3 c. stirred whole wheat flour	2 c. milk
¾ c. all-purpose flour	¾ c. vegetable oil
½ c. wheat germ	½ c. honey
1 c. sugar	½ c. dark corn syrup
1 c. nonfat dry milk	2 c. raisins
2 tsp. baking powder	6 oz. snipped dry apricots (1⅓ c.)
1 tsp. salt	1 c. roasted, salted sunflower seeds
1 tsp. ground cinnamon	
4 eggs	

In large bowl stir together whole wheat flour, all-purpose flour, wheat germ, sugar, dry milk, baking powder, salt and cinnamon.

In smaller bowl beat eggs; blend in milk, oil, honey and corn syrup. Add to dry ingredients, stirring just until moistened. Stir in raisins, apricots and sunflower seeds. Spread in greased 15×10×1″ jelly roll pan.

Bake in 350° oven 45 minutes. Makes 3 dozen bars.

PEANUT-DATE BALLS

Dates help sweeten these no-bake confections, a great substitute for candy. Chopped peanuts add crispness and flavor

1½ c. peanut butter
1 (8 oz.) pkg. chopped dates
½ c. flaked coconut
1 tsp. lemon juice

¾ c. sifted confectioners
   sugar
1 c. finely chopped peanuts

Stir together peanut butter, dates, coconut and lemon juice. Blend in sugar. Cover and chill at least 1 hour. Shape heaping teaspoonfuls of mixture in balls. Roll in chopped peanuts. Makes about 3½ dozen.

FRUITCAKE SQUARES

Instead of fruit cake, serve holiday guests these subtly orange-flavored snack bars with hot coffee or Friendship Punch. Raisins, dates, nuts and eggs contribute nutrients

1½ c. dates, coarsely
   chopped
1 c. light raisins
1 c. dark raisins
1 c. coarsely chopped nuts
½ c. halved candied
   cherries
½ c. chopped candied
   pineapple

1 c. sifted all-purpose flour
1½ tsp. salt
4 eggs
1 c. brown sugar, firmly
   packed
1 tblsp. grated orange peel
1 tsp. vanilla
½ c. sugar
¼ c. orange juice

Combine fruits and nuts. Stir together flour and salt. Sprinkle fruit with ¼ c. flour mixture and stir to coat.

Beat eggs until frothy. Beat in brown sugar, orange peel and vanilla. Stir in dry ingredients and fruit mixture, mixing well. Spread in greased 15×10×1″ jelly roll pan.

Bake in 325° oven 30 to 35 minutes or until lightly browned.

In small saucepan combine sugar and orange juice. Cook, stirring constantly, until mixture comes to a boil and sugar is dissolved. Brush over warm baked cookies. Cut in bars. Makes about 4 dozen.

APPLESAUCE OATMEAL DROPS

A big recipe for dough you can keep in the refrigerator three days. When the spirit moves you—or your teen-age children— bake up a batch of these spicy, moist, soft cookies

1 c. shortening	1 tsp. salt
2 c. brown sugar, firmly packed	1 tsp. ground cinnamon
	½ tsp. baking powder
2 eggs	½ tsp. ground cloves
½ c. milk	½ tsp. ground nutmeg
1 (16 oz.) can applesauce (2 c.)	1 c. quick-cooking rolled oats
2½ c. sifted all-purpose flour	1 c. raisins
	½ c. chopped nuts
1 tsp. baking soda	

Cream together shortening and brown sugar until light and fluffy. Add eggs, beating thoroughly. Stir in milk and applesauce.

Sift together flour, soda, salt, cinnamon, baking powder, cloves and nutmeg. Stir in rolled oats. Add to creamed mixture, stirring until blended. Fold in raisins and nuts. Cover and chill at least 2 hours. Drop by heaping teaspoonfuls on greased baking sheet 2" apart.

Bake in 400° oven 10 to 12 minutes or until lightly browned. Cool on racks. Makes 7 to 8 dozen cookies.

UP-TO-DATE CAKES

CRANBERRY CALICO CAKE

This is the kind of cake that starts a recipe exchange whenever women meet. Dotted with dark dates and red berries and topped with a shiny orange glaze

3 c. sifted all-purpose flour	1 tsp. grated orange peel
2½ tsp. baking powder	¼ c. milk
½ tsp. salt	¼ c. orange juice
½ c. butter or margarine	2 c. sliced cranberries
½ c. shortening	1 c. chopped dates
1½ c. sugar	Orange Glaze (recipe
4 eggs	follows)

Sift together flour, baking powder and salt.

Cream together butter, shortening and sugar until light and fluffy. Add eggs, one at a time, beating well after each addition. Stir in orange peel.

Combine milk and orange juice. Add to creamed mixture alternately with sifted dry ingredients. Fold in cranberries and dates. Spread in well greased 10" tube pan.

Bake in 350° oven 80 to 85 minutes or until cake tester inserted in cake comes out clean. Let cool in pan 10 minutes. Turn out on rack; cool completely. Spread with Orange Glaze.

Orange Glaze: In small mixer bowl combine 2 tblsp. softened butter or margarine, 1 tsp. grated orange peel, dash of salt, 2 c. sifted confectioners sugar and 2½ tblsp. orange juice. Beat until well blended.

APPLESAUCE CAKE

Soy flour boosts the protein in this country favorite laced with nuts and raisins, but no one will taste the soy

1½ c. unsifted all-purpose flour	½ c. shortening
1 c. stirred soy flour	1 (16 oz.) can applesauce (2 c.)
1½ tsp. salt	3 eggs
1½ tsp. baking soda	1 c. raisins
¼ tsp. baking powder	½ c. chopped nuts
1 tsp. ground cinnamon	Cream Cheese Frosting (recipe follows)
½ tsp. ground nutmeg	
½ tsp. ground cloves	

In large mixer bowl stir together flours, salt, baking soda, baking powder and spices until well blended. Add shortening and applesauce. Beat at low speed 1 minute, scraping sides and bottom of bowl constantly. Beat at medium speed 2 minutes more, scraping sides of bowl frequently. Add eggs. Beat at medium speed an additional 2 minutes. By hand fold in raisins and nuts. Spread batter in greased and floured 13×9×2" baking pan.

Bake in 350° oven 45 to 50 minutes or until cake's surface springs back when lightly touched. Cool and frost with Cream

Cheese Frosting. For fewer calories, cut frosting recipe in half or omit frosting and sprinkle cake with confectioners sugar.

Cream Cheese Frosting: Cream together ½ c. butter or margarine, 1 (8 oz.) pkg. cream cheese, softened, and 1 tsp. vanilla. Gradually beat in 1 lb. confectioners sugar (sifted if lumpy). If mixture is too thick to spread, add a small amount of milk.

ORANGE SPONGE CAKE

No one ever baked a more handsome or tastier sponge cake than this. Nutritious soy flour is the unusual ingredient

⅔ c. unsifted all-purpose flour	6 egg whites
⅔ c. stirred soy flour	1 tsp. cream of tartar
½ tsp. baking powder	6 egg yolks
½ tsp. salt	2 tsp. grated orange peel
1½ c. sugar	¼ c. orange juice
	Confectioners sugar

Stir together flours, baking powder, salt and 1 c. sugar.

In large mixer bowl combine egg whites and cream of tartar. Beat until soft peaks form. Gradually add remaining ½ c. sugar, beating until stiff peaks form.

In another bowl beat egg yolks until thick and lemon colored. Beat in orange peel and juice.

By hand stir flour mixture into egg yolks; beat ½ minute. Fold into egg whites just until blended. Pour into 10″ ungreased tube pan.

Bake in 375° oven 45 to 50 minutes. Remove from oven and invert pan on funnel or bottle until cool, at least 1 hour, before removing from pan. Sift a little confectioners sugar over the cake before cutting.

SPICY LEMON PRUNE CAKE

Prunes supply iron and other minerals while sweetening and flavoring this cake. The cheese glaze is the perfect topping, but skip it if you're counting calories. Freeze unfrosted

1 (12 oz.) pkg. pitted prunes	¾ c. butter or margarine
1½ c. water	1½ c. sugar
3 c. sifted all-purpose flour	4 eggs
2 tsp. baking powder	1 tblsp. grated lemon peel
1 tsp. baking soda	1 tsp. vanilla
¾ tsp. ground cinnamon	1 c. chopped nuts
½ tsp. salt	Lemon Cheese Glaze
⅛ tsp. ground nutmeg	(recipe follows)
⅛ tsp. ground cloves	

In saucepan cook prunes in water until tender, about 5 minutes. Whirl prunes and water in blender or force through sieve. Mixture should measure 2 c.; add more water if necessary. Let prune purée cool while measuring and preparing other ingredients.

Sift together dry ingredients.

In large mixer bowl cream butter and sugar until light and fluffy. Add eggs and beat until mixture is a pale yellow color, about 3 minutes.

By hand stir in lemon peel and vanilla. Add dry ingredients alternately with prune purée, mixing just enough to blend. Fold in nuts. Spread in greased and floured 13×9×2″ baking pan.

Bake in 350° oven 40 to 45 minutes or until cake's surface

springs back when lightly touched. Cool on rack. If desired, spread with Lemon Cheese Glaze.

Lemon Cheese Glaze: Blend together 1 (3 oz.) pkg. cream cheese and 2 tblsp. lemon juice. Beat in 2½ c. sifted confectioners sugar and 1 tblsp. light cream. Stir in 1 tsp. grated lemon peel.

OATMEAL CAKE

Taste testers gave this homespun cake an A-1 rating, or as the teen-agers said: "You 'aced' with this cake." It is good without frosting, but add one if you are not calorie saving

½ c. boiling water
½ c. quick-cooking rolled oats
¾ c. milk
1¼ c. sifted all-purpose flour
1 tsp. salt
½ tsp. baking powder
½ tsp. baking soda

½ tsp. ground cinnamon
¼ tsp. ground cloves
½ c. raisins
½ c. chopped nuts
½ c. butter or margarine
¼ c. sugar
1 c. brown sugar, firmly packed
2 eggs

Pour boiling water over rolled oats. Add milk, stirring to remove any lumps; cool.

Sift together flour, salt, baking powder, baking soda and spices. Stir in raisins and nuts.

Cream together butter and sugars until light and fluffy. Add eggs, blending until well blended. Stir in cooled oatmeal mixture. Add dry ingredients by thirds, mixing thoroughly after each addition. Spread into greased and floured 9″ square pan.

Bake in 350° oven 50 to 55 minutes. Sprinkle with sifted confectioners sugar or spread with confectioners sugar frosting, if desired. Makes 9 servings.

HIGH NUTRITION CAKE

*An excellent snack cake, a cross between cake and bar cookies.
It is correctly named, and it tastes wonderful*

½ c. peanut butter
⅓ c. butter or margarine
1 c. sugar
2 eggs
2 tsp. vanilla
2 c. high protein cereal
  flakes
1 c. mashed bananas (about
  2 large)

¾ c. milk
2 c. sifted all-purpose flour
½ tsp. salt
2 tsp. baking powder
¼ tsp. baking soda
1½ c. chopped peanuts

Cream together peanut butter and butter. Add sugar, beating
until light and fluffy. Beat in eggs, one at a time. Beat in vanilla.
Stir in cereal flakes.

Combine banana with milk. Sift together flour, salt, baking
powder and baking soda. Add flour mixture to creamed mixture
alternately with banana and milk. Fold in peanuts. Spread in
greased and floured 13×9×2″ baking pan.

Bake in 350° oven 35 to 40 minutes or until cake's surface
springs back when lightly touched. Makes 16 cake servings, 24
bars.

ONE-CRUST PIES
AND OTHER DESSERT SNACKS

SWEET POTATO PECAN PIE

Flute the edges of the pie shell high to hold the generous filling. Superior taste and many nutrients make this special

1½ c. puréed fresh or canned sweet potatoes	¼ tsp. ground cloves
	½ tsp. salt
2 eggs	1¼ c. milk
¾ c. sugar	1 (9″) unbaked pie shell,
1 tsp. ground cinnamon	edges fluted high
½ tsp. ground ginger	½ c. chopped pecans

If fresh sweet potatoes are used, cook in boiling water, peel and put through a food mill or sieve, or purée in blender.

In large bowl beat eggs. Stir in sweet potato purée, sugar, spices and salt. Blend in milk. Pour into pie shell. Sprinkle with pecans.

Bake in 400° oven 50 minutes or until knife inserted halfway between center and edges comes out clean.

NEW-FASHIONED PUMPKIN PIE

A different version of pumpkin chiffon pie, made with yogurt. Its refreshing filling is on the tart side

1 envelope unflavored
  gelatin
¼ c. water
1 (16 oz.) can pumpkin
1 c. honey
1 tsp. ground cinnamon
½ tsp. ground ginger

¼ tsp. ground cloves
½ tsp. salt
1 (8 oz.) carton spiced apple
  yogurt
1 (9″) baked pastry shell
⅓ c. chopped pecans
  (optional)

Soften gelatin in water in small saucepan; place over low heat, stirring constantly until dissolved. Stir into pumpkin. Stir in honey, spices, salt and yogurt. Turn into pastry shell. Sprinkle with pecans. Refrigerate until set.

PIONEER APRICOT PRUNE PIE

The dried fruits provide superlative flavors, vitamin A, iron and other minerals. Pioneer women sprinkled top of this tart pie with confectioners sugar, but you can do better: Dip into the freezer for scoops of vanilla ice cream

1 (12 oz.) pkg. pitted prunes
1 c. dried apricots
1 tblsp. grated lemon peel
3 c. water
3 tblsp. cornstarch
½ c. water

¼ c. sugar
1 tsp. ground cinnamon
Dash of salt
1 (9″) baked pastry shell
1 qt. vanilla ice cream

In saucepan combine prunes, apricots, lemon peel and 3 c. water. Bring to a boil; reduce heat and simmer, covered, 15 minutes.

Blend together cornstarch and ½ c. water. Add to fruit mixture. Cook, stirring constantly, until mixture thickens and bubbles. Stir in sugar, cinnamon and salt.

Cool. Spread into pastry shell and chill. To serve, cut in wedges and top with ice cream. Makes 8 servings.

PINEAPPLE CHEESE PIE

Tastes like cheese cake—equally delicious but not so rich

1½ c. graham cracker crumbs (about 20 crackers)	⅓ c. butter or margarine
	Cottage Cheese Filling
	Pineapple Topping (recipes
3 tblsp. sugar	follow)

Combine crumbs and sugar. Blend in butter. Press into 9" pie pan. Bake in 350° oven 10 minutes. Cool.

Spoon Cottage Cheese Filling into crust. Chill until firm, about 3 hours. Top with Pineapple Topping. Chill until served. Makes 6 to 8 servings.

COTTAGE CHEESE FILLING

¾ c. sugar	1 tblsp. grated lemon peel
1 envelope unflavored gelatin	1 tblsp. grated orange peel
	½ tsp. vanilla
¼ tsp. salt	2 c. creamed cottage cheese, sieved
2 eggs	
1 c. milk	

In saucepan combine sugar, gelatin and salt. Beat in eggs until blended. Stir in milk. Cook over medium heat, stirring constantly, until mixture thickens and coats a metal spoon. Remove from heat; stir in lemon and orange peels and vanilla. Chill until mixture mounds when dropped from a spoon.

Combine with cheese in large mixer bowl. Beat at high speed until light and fluffy, about 5 minutes. If filling is thin, refrigerate 10 minutes before spooning into crust.

PINEAPPLE TOPPING

1 tblsp. sugar	1 tblsp. lemon juice
2 tsp. cornstarch	Few drops yellow food color
1 (8 oz.) can crushed pineapple	

In small saucepan combine sugar and cornstarch. Stir in undrained pineapple, lemon juice and food color. Cook over medium heat, stirring constantly, until mixture bubbles and is translucent. Cool thoroughly. Spread over pie.

LEMON FLUFF PIE

This pie is an adaptation of the old-time Pennsylvania Dutch lemon sponge pie. Like its forerunners, filling is as light as thistledown and lemon flavor is full-bodied

6 egg yolks	6 egg whites
½ c. sugar	3 tblsp. sugar
⅛ tsp. salt	1 (9″) baked pastry shell
1½ tsp. grated lemon peel	2 tblsp. shredded coconut
⅓ c. lemon juice	(optional)

In small mixer bowl beat egg yolks, ½ c. sugar and salt until thick and lemon colored. Beat in lemon peel and juice. Turn into top of double boiler. Cook over boiling water, stirring constantly, until mixture is very thick, about 8 minutes. Cool slightly.

Beat egg whites until frothy. Add 3 tblsp. sugar gradually, beating until stiff peaks form. Fold into lemon mixture. Spoon into baked pastry. Sprinkle coconut over the top.

Bake in 350° oven 20 minutes. Cool and cut carefully with serrated knife.

SWEDISH APPLE PUDDING

Graham crackers were named for Sylvester Graham, an eighteenth century vegetarian and reformer who advocated the use of coarsely ground whole wheat flour. They add nourishment to this pudding made with applesauce and topped with a smooth, velvety custard sauce

3 c. graham cracker crumbs
  (about 40 crackers)
½ c. melted butter or
  margarine
2 (16 oz.) cans applesauce
  (4 c.)

1 tsp. ground cinnamon
Custard Sauce (recipe
  follows)

In skillet combine graham cracker crumbs and butter. Cook over medium heat 5 minutes, stirring constantly to prevent scorching. Spread ⅓ of crumbs in bottom of an 8″ square pan. Carefully spread 2 c. (or 1 can) applesauce over crumbs. Sprinkle with ½ tsp. cinnamon. Repeat layers of crumbs, applesauce and cinnamon. Top with remaining crumbs.

Bake in 350° oven 45 minutes. Serve warm or cold with Custard Sauce. Makes 6 to 8 servings.

CUSTARD SAUCE

2 eggs, slightly beaten   1 c. light cream or milk
⅓ c. sugar   1 tsp. vanilla
Dash of salt

In small saucepan combine eggs, sugar and salt. Stir in cream or milk. Cook over low heat, stirring constantly, until mixture thickens and coats a spoon. Remove from heat. Add vanilla. Chill. Makes about 1⅓ cups.

APPLE CAKE DESSERT

Cake, soft custard and apples make an old-fashioned country dessert. The frozen cake is convenient—or you can bake a sponge cake or pound cake from scratch or from a mix

2 qts. sliced, unpeeled   3 tblsp. sugar
  apples (about 2 lbs.)   Dash of salt
2 tblsp. water   1½ c. milk
¾ c. sugar   ½ tsp. vanilla
½ tsp. ground cinnamon   1 (10¾ oz.) pkg. frozen
1 tsp. grated lemon peel   pound cake, thawed
2 eggs, slightly beaten   ½ c. heavy cream, whipped

In large saucepan cook apples, covered, with water until tender. Put through food mill or sieve. Stir in ¾ c. sugar, cinnamon and lemon peel. Chill.

In top of double boiler combine eggs, 3 tblsp. sugar, salt and milk. Cook over boiling water, stirring constantly, until mixture thickens and coats a spoon. Remove from heat and set in bowl of ice water. Stir in vanilla. Chill thoroughly.

Cut cake into 16 slices. Put 8 slices in bottom of an 8″ square pan, cutting slices to fit if necessary. Top with half of applesauce and half of custard. Repeat with second layers of cake, applesauce and custard. Chill 4 to 8 hours. Before serving, spread top with whipped cream. Makes 6 to 8 servings.

CHOCOLATE PEANUT SPREAD

To pacify a sweet tooth, try this honeyed protein spread. On a graham cracker, it adds up to about 65 calories; on a smaller whole wheat cracker, about 42 calories

1 c. peanut butter, smooth	**3 tblsp. cocoa**
or crunchy	**1 tsp. vanilla**
⅔ c. honey	

Combine all ingredients. Serve as a spread on graham or whole wheat crackers. Makes about 1⅓ cups.

There are more good desserts in other recipes in this book: consult Index for page numbers.

In Chapter 2, "SNACK BUT STAY SLIM"
         Banana Popsicles
         Blueberry Sicles
         Butterscotch Pumpkin Pudding
         Cranberry Orange Sherbet
         Diet Apricot Dessert
         Peaches with Spicy Yogurt
         Peachy Cheese Dessert

Strawberry Buttermilk Sherbet
Three Fruit Sherbet
Wintertime Minted Fruit Cup

In Chapter 5, "MILK . . . STILL THE DEPENDABLE"
Apple Torte
High-Hat Banana Custards
Maple Custard
Strawberry Angel Dessert

Chapter 8

MAKE SNACKS COUNT
IN THE DAY'S MEALS

What thoughtful mother doesn't want to feed her family well? Meals must taste good, but more and more we are beginning to realize that they also need to be nutritious, to provide the best opportunities for growth, development and health. Snacks can be very helpful in achieving a day's optimum nutrition.

A great deal of the responsibility for your family's health lies with you (or whomever in the family does most of the grocery shopping and meal getting). You're pretty much the monitor of the food which comes into the house and how it is delivered to the family members either in meals or snacks.

The first step is to decide on the foods you'll be serving during the day. It isn't enough to plan just one or possibly two of the meals at a time. Meals and snacks cannot be separated when you think about the foods your family needs.

For good health, each family member's food intake must be judged on the basis of the entire day's intake—including the snacks, whether eaten at home or away from home. It is *all* the food eaten that gives the true picture of how good the daily diet is nutritionally.

To be a good monitor, you need to know how much food different members of your family should eat, based on their growth and requirements—these vary by age, sex and activity. You also need to know what they're eating each day. While you can see what they eat when they sit down at your table, it may require the utmost tact to find out what they're *really* eating away from home.

Every body needs all the same nutrients throughout life but in different amounts. Proportionately greater amounts are needed for growth of a body than just for its upkeep. Boys and men need more than girls and women. Large people need more than small people. Active people need more food energy than inactive ones and food energy needs decline as people grow older. People recovering from illness need more than healthy people.

One of the purposes of this book is to help you choose and prepare snacks for your family to supplement meals at home and away from home, so that the total intake for each member will equal a diet for good health.

Chapters in this book are organized to make it easy for you to locate the kind of snack foods that individual family members might need. For example, Chapter 5 gave you ideas for milk snacks to fix for someone who's not drinking his milk at mealtimes.

The key to successful snacking is knowing what the snacker needs most. If your school's lunch program menus are published, you have some idea of what your children are eating . . . though you may still have to ask—did they actually eat it? Ask questions, not for condemnation, but for information.

Convince everyone of the fact that the kind and the amount of food is important to growth and well-being and performance *on a day-to-day basis*. Help each child take pride in assuming responsibility (appropriate to his age) for his food choices for good health.

Reassure your family that you believe eating should be enjoyable. Nutrition does not mean eating food you do not like, simply because it is good for you. If a child honestly doesn't like a particular food, there is sure to be a nutritive substitute. A mother's role needs to be supportive in helping the children develop good food habits. That means having snacks available that will be nutritionally valuable—and that children will enjoy.

If you think of food by the day rather than by individual meals, you will find it easier to give each family member his full day's quota of nutrients. It is not essential that a child drink orange juice at breakfast; he can get his RDA (Recommended Daily Allowance) of vitamin C in some other way at some other time of the day. The important thing is to plan each day's food —meals *and* snacks—to get it all together.

Nutrition intake needs daily examination; however, it soon becomes automatic. A conscientious monitor will spot a nutritional shortage and usually can make it up the same day rather than allow it to build up. For example:

If a child averages only a cup of milk a day instead of the two or three cups he needs, try to find ways to step up milk intake itself (flavored milk drinks, etc.), or make available snacks that would include milk products in some form.

Here are some other typical eating patterns that can be improved by adopting good snack habits:

Older children who may eat several meals or snacks a week at fast-food restaurants are undoubtedly missing some of the fruits and vegetables they need to supply vitamins and minerals. And fiber. Encourage them to snack on fruit and vegetable snacks from Chapter 3. Have fruit juice and/or refrigerator salads available when they get home.

An active teen-age boy has high requirements for both energy and nutrients. While he may eat perfectly balanced meals at your table, he may need additional main-dish snacks from Chapter 6 to keep up his energy and permit his optimum growth.

The husband you describe as "a meat-and-potatoes man" is

cheating himself of well-being if he doesn't eat a bit more adventurously. Can you provide between-meal snacks containing fruits, vegetables and milk products?

And what about you? It is easy for the homemaker, who's busy taking care of everyone else, to skip meals when other family members are not present . . . and to nibble, not eat, before, during and after regular family meals. If you're sewing on buttons when the family's eating a good breakfast, take time for a midmorning snack—make it fruit and protein, not a sweet bun.

SAMPLE MENUS THAT MAKE SNACKS PART OF EACH DAY'S EATING

People enjoy snacks so much, they usually welcome them with enthusiasm. Menus in this section are splendid examples of what an excellent tool they can be to meal planners.

First, in this chapter, we suggest some snack-*meals* for anyone who doesn't make it home for supper. Perhaps only one member of the family will be so busy with school activities or job that he can't be home at the regular mealtime. Or several people in the family circle may occasionally have to eat dinner at different hours. Snacks are a practical solution for off-hour meals. And there are an increasing number of households where snack meals are favored because they taste good and are fast to fix and eat.

Here are some good examples of planned mini-meals that supply essential nutrients. A star (*) marks recipes that appear in this book; consult the Index for page numbers.

Ground Beef Mini-Meal*
Whole Wheat Bread*   Butter
Pea-nutty Cookies*
Milk

Chicken Vegetable Soup*
Marinated Tomatoes*
Cottage Cheese Muffins*   Honey
Maple Custard*
Milk

Individual Pizzas*
Vegetable Marinade*
Cantaloupe Wedges
Granola Cookies*
Milk

Italian Chef's Salad Mix*
Zucchini Nut Bread*   Butter
Pineapple Cheese Pie*
Milk

Grilled Tortilla Cheese Sandwiches*
Mexican Bean Salad*
Yogurt Fruit Combo*
Milk

Individual Chicken Casserole*
Succotash Salad*
Bread   Butter
Chocolate Ice Cream Soda*
Milk

Basic Hamburgers* on Whole Wheat Buns*
Blue Cheese Tomatoes
Italian Potato Salad*
Applesauce Cake*
Milk

Stuffed Franks*
Refrigerator Carrot Salad*
Rhubarb Sauce
Oatmeal Cake*
Milk

SNACKS AS NUTRITION BOOSTERS

You can choose snacks to make up for some nutrient missing from your day's menus. A citrus-based punch in the evening, with cookies, seems more like a treat than orange juice for breakfast. And it fills the daily requirement for vitamin C just as well.

Snacks make it possible for you to prepare family meals and still cater to individual needs or preferences. While we all require the same nutrients, the amounts each person needs depends on age, sex, size, activity, etc. It is easier for you to add a snack, or substitute a snack for food refused, than to fix a second dinner menu.

Here are some menus which illustrate how neatly snacks fit

into a day's food blueprint—either for the whole family, or to
supplement individual needs:

TYPICAL DAY

Breakfast	*Lunch*
Stewed Prunes	Beefburgers
Poached Eggs	Buttered Peas
Toasted English Muffins	Chocolate Cupcake
Coffee	Milk
Milk	

Dinner
Pot Roast and Gravy
Pot-Roasted Potatoes, Carrots and Onions
Cherry Crisp
Milk

Snack booster: Golden Grape Punch* to supply vitamin C and
Oatmeal Cookies

TYPICAL DAY

Breakfast	*Lunch*
Cantaloupe Quarters	Bacon and Tomato Sandwiches
Scrambled Eggs	Dilly Cheese-Stuffed Celery*
Buttered Toast	Brownies
Coffee	Milk

Dinner
Grilled Hamburgers on Sour Dough Bread
Corn on the Cob
Tossed Mixed Greens with Blue Cheese Dressing
Butterscotch Sundaes
Iced Tea

Snack booster (for children): Vanilla Milk Shake* for extra
calcium

TYPICAL DAY

Breakfast
Grapefruit Half
High Protein Cereal Flakes
  Milk
Coffee

Lunch
Baked Beans and Franks
Cherry Gelatin Salad
Toasted Buns
Chocolate Ice Cream Cones

Dinner
Oven-Fried Fish Fillets   Lemon Wedges
Creamed Potatoes and Peas
Pickled Beet-Onion Ring Salad
Golden Layer Cake with Caramel Frosting
Coffee or Milk

Snack booster: Dilled Cheese Dip* for calcium, with Carrot and Green Pepper Strips to supply vitamin A

MEATLESS DAY

Breakfast
Stewed Apricots and Prunes
Granola Cereal   Milk
Coffee

Lunch
Creamed Eggs on Toasted
  English Muffins
Citrus Salad
Sunflower Refrigerator
  Cookies*
Milk

Dinner
Macaroni-Cheese Salad
Italian Green Beans
Carrot Slaw*
Herb-Buttered French Bread
High Nutrition Cake*

Snack booster: Peanut Cereal Snack Mix* for extra protein

FOR CALORIE COUNTERS

Breakfast	*Lunch*
Orange Juice	Slim Jim Cheeseburgers*
Poached Egg on Toast	Snacker's Tomato Soup*
Coffee	Honeydew Wedge
	Skim Milk

Dinner
Broiled Chicken
Grilled Herbed Tomato Halves
Summer Squash
Minted Fresh Fruit Cup
Skim Milk

Snack booster: Blueberry Sicles* for a low-calorie treat with some calcium and protein value

FOR GOLDEN AGERS

Breakfast	*Lunch*
Grapefruit Half	Vegetable-Beef Soup
Hot Oatmeal Milk	Crisp Crackers
Coffee	Cup Custard

Dinner
Broiled Halibut, Lemon Wedges
Creamed Spinach
Whole Wheat Roll, Butter
Fruit Cup and Cookie
Milk

Snack booster: Vegetable Dippers with Zippy Beef Dip* for extra nutrients without excess calories

FOR ACTIVE FARMERS

Breakfast	*Lunch*
Orange Juice	Baked Tuna Casserole
Sausage	Parsley Buttered Carrots
Buttermilk Griddle Cakes	Hot Rolls Butter
Syrup	Applesauce
Coffee	Milk

Dinner
Braised Pork Chops
Sour Cream Potatoes
Stewed Tomatoes
Corn Bread   Butter
Relish Tray
Deep Dish Peach Pie
Beverage

Snack booster (morning): Pecan Roll* and Mexican Chocolate*
(afternoon): Honey-Raisin Cookies* Ice Tea
for energy and some extra nutrients

FOR MORE BULK

Breakfast	*Lunch*
Pineapple Juice	Tomatoes Stuffed with Tuna
Hot Whole Wheat Cereal	Salad
Milk	Bran Raisin Muffins*
Coffee	Butter
	Apple Cookie
	Milk

Dinner
Hamburger Stroganoff   Brown Rice
Buttered Green Beans
Tossed Salad
Four-Grain Bread*   Butter
Fresh Fruit Cup with Raspberry Yogurt
Milk

Snack booster: Five-Cup Snack Mix* for extra fiber

SNACK SAMPLER FOR THE HOSTESS

When it's time for refreshments, a hostess can count on snacks to win approval and compliments. Here are suggestions for evening specials:

Orange Sponge Cake*
Friendship Punch*

Apple Cake Dessert*
Coffee

Party Tuna Spread* and Crackers
Spiced Nuts*
Dilled Cheese Dip* and Vegetable Dippers
Cranberry Apple Pitcher Punch*

You might serve the following interesting (and nutritious) breads with morning coffee or afternoon tea to women visitors:

Kaffee Klatch
Cinnamon Rolls*
Date Oatmeal Crescent Rolls*
Coffee

Informal Tea
Toasted English Oat Muffins*
Banana Nut Loaf Cheese Sandwiches*
Spiced Tea*

Snacks for tots and teen-agers include popular ice cream to furnish some of the additional calcium that youngsters need:

Small Fry Treats
Banana Cookies*
Double Chocolate Shake*

Teen Night
Sloppy Joe Barbecue*
French Onion Dip*   Vegetable Dippers
Chocolate Peppermint Shake*

Chapter 9

GROCERY SHOPPING
FOR GOOD NUTRITION

Nutrients in the right assortments and amounts are the ingredients that build good health and well-being.

But we don't eat nutrients as such; we eat *food* which supplies the nutrients. We don't grow nutrients as such; we grow *food*. Neither do we need to buy nutrients as such; we buy *food*.

Scientists know of at least fifty nutrients which the body must have. Each has specific jobs to do in the building, upkeep and operation of the body, jobs which cannot be done by any other nutrient. An extra supply of one nutrient cannot make up for a shortage of another.

Actually, interdependence is the name of the game when it comes to describing the work of the nutrients. In addition to their specific jobs, nutrients work together to perform some services for the body which no one nutrient can do alone. Nor can any nutrient do its own special work in isolation. For example, bones and teeth are not built by calcium alone, no matter how much calcium-containing foods you consume.

You don't need to know the names and functions of the individual vitamins, minerals, amino acids, fatty acids and starches and sugars. But you do need to know the kinds of foods you can depend on to supply them. Here variety is the key to health. No single food and no group of similar foods contain all the nutrients in significant amounts.

Most foods supply more than one nutrient. Some common foods contain relatively large amounts of one or more nutrients, and smaller amounts of others. For instance, milk and milk products are a prime source of calcium and riboflavin but also supply other minerals and vitamins as well as protein. Dark leafy green vegetables are a prime source of vitamin A, but also supply iron, vitamin C, thiamin, etc.

Because several nutrients are likely to occur together in food, often it is sufficient to mention just the prime one and follow it with the phrase "other nutrients" or "other vitamins and minerals," to indicate additional nutritive value.

For a good many of our nutrients, there is no outstanding food source; therefore we must depend on smaller amounts from many food sources. Just another reason for the need for *variety* in our diets.*

With this brief background you can understand why the important word in shopping for food, or planning the day's—and week's—menus, is VARIETY.

Questions and Answers

Q. Is water a nutrient?

A. We don't always think of water as a nutrient, but it is most

---

* A fund of information makes the subject of nutrition more interesting to some people. If you want to read more about the nutrients and how they work together in your body, there are several books and publications available. A good one (even easy to read by children) is "Food Is More Than Just Something to Eat," *free* from Consumer Information Center, Pueblo, Colorado 81009. The USDA Home & Garden Bulletin ⚡1, "Family Fare" also describes the nutrients. It is $1 from the Superintendent of Documents, U. S. Government Printing Office, Washington, D.C. 20402. The 1969 USDA Yearbook, *Food For Us All*, has a good section on "Your Basic Food Needs: Nutrients for Life, Growth," and a section on healthier snacking, too. Look in your library for this book, or contact your Congressman. Your Extension Service home economist will also have information for you.

important. You can get along for days, even weeks, without food but only a few days without water. You can't make use of the other nutrients in food without water to dissolve them and carry them through the intestinal wall and into the blood stream. Water also carries waste out of the body and helps to regulate body temperature.

Q. How much water should a person drink?

A. While you could exist on four glasses of water a day, a more practical minimum is eight glasses. Part of this water can be in the form of other liquids—milk, coffee, fruit juices, etc.

Q. Many packages and cans of food carry nutrition information on the label. How should I use this information?

A. Nutrition labeling may tell you more (or less) than you want to know about foods. It can be a useful tool for getting information and making certain comparisons among foods of similar composition and use. But it's easy to misuse nutrition labeling. It can put you on a collision course with frustration or misinformation, or give you a false sense of security.

Q. What nutrition information is supposed to be on the label?

A. Nutrition labeling is voluntary except when a nutrient is added or a special nutritional or dietetic claim is made for the product, and then the label must provide nutritional information. Many (but not all) processed foods now carry a nutrition information panel. When it appears it must state the following:
   • Serving size and the number of servings in the container
   • Calorie value per serving
   • Protein, carbohydrate and fat content in grams per serving. (This tells you where the calories come from.)
   • The rest of the information is expressed in percentages of U.S. RDA. The U. S. Recommended Dietary Allowance of a nutrient is the highest amount recommended daily for good health at almost every age. Thus the label tells you that a serving supplies X-per cent of the U.S. RDA for the following

nutrients: protein, vitamin A, vitamin C, thiamin, riboflavin, niacin, and calcium and iron.

Q. Can I use nutrition labeling as a guide in menu planning?

A. No. You need many types of foods to make up a good diet. Not all foods are labeled with nutritional information—fresh vegetables and meat, for example. Labeling was never intended to serve as a guide in menu planning, nor as a shopping guide.

Q. Then what is the value of nutrition labeling?

A. Here are two ways to make good use of nutrition labeling.

(1) You can check labels to see how different forms of the same food may vary. For example, compare a can of plain white potatoes with a can of French fried potato sticks to see how many calories the fat adds. The label on potatoes au gratin will show differences in the nutrient content of calcium resulting from the addition of milk and cheese; it may also show less iron because of the displacement of part of the potato with milk.

(2) You can use labels to compare foods that might be used interchangeably in your meals or snacks. For example, you can compare values for fresh whole milk with those for chocolate drink, cream cheese with American cheese, tuna with peanut butter, orange juice with tomato juice.

But note: Nutrition labeling is not helpful in comparing different types of foods. You don't learn anything useful trying to compare milk with canned green beans, for example. Milk supplies certain nutrients to the diet; green beans supply other nutrients. The two foods are not interchangeable.

Q. How is nutrition labeling misused or misinterpreted?

A. One error that consumers make is comparing most foods on the basis of protein content. Such preoccupation with protein is detrimental to most meal and snack planning. Suppose you're considering bean soup or canned luncheon meat for a noon meal. You choose the meat because it has higher protein value, even though it costs more. Yet you plan family meals and snacks to provide liberal amounts of milk, eggs, cheese and meat. You don't need the extra protein in the canned meat.

Labeling may also lead you to buy a product on the basis of its high nutrient, forgetting that your total meal planning already provides plenty of that nutrient. For example, suppose your family likes applesauce, but you decide on stewed tomatoes because it is higher in vitamins C and A. But your family is already getting its daily need of vitamin C from orange juice for breakfast, and of vitamin A from carrot sticks in packed lunches.

Another misconception concerns the U.S. RDA. Many people believe that reaching 100 per cent is necessary and/or sufficient for every family member. The U.S. RDA is the highest amount recommended at almost every age. Most family members require considerably less of each nutrient to meet their needs and still have some overages. For instance, eight-year-olds need only about 66 per cent, not 100 per cent, of the U.S. RDAs—except for calcium, of which they need 100 per cent. Teen-agers and nursing mothers need considerably more than the U.S. RDA for calcium—that's why extra milk is recommended for them.

SHOPPER'S GUIDE TO GOOD EATING

There are some 8,000 or more items in a large food store today: fresh, frozen, canned and packaged foods in such variety and quantity that an adequate diet is within the reach of every

American who has the money to buy it—and the knowledge to select it.

Today in our own country, poor eating is more likely to stem from ignorance than from poverty . . . ignorance and/or carelessness. Many mothers try to give their families the right foods in the recommended amounts, but they lose control when children snack away from home or refuse part of their meals at school.

In the paragraphs that introduce recipe chapters in this book, you will find all kinds of ideas for promoting nutritious snacks to your family using good psychology—and good-tasting food.

The next few pages will tell you which foods to promote especially. So, come push an imaginary shopping cart through the aisles of the grocery store and collect the food to feed your family for their good health but also for their enjoyment.

FRUITS AND VEGETABLES

Often when you walk into a food store you see first the fresh fruit and vegetable section with its orderly display of colorful, inviting products. The assortment will vary with the season. Most of the time there will be: citrus fruits, especially oranges and grapefruit; dark green vegetables such as broccoli, spinach, and other dark green leafies; deep yellow vegetables such as carrots. More seasonally, there will be sweet potatoes, winter squash and pumpkin and deep yellow fruits such as apricots and cantaloupe.

If you buy enough citrus fruit for a serving per person per day, you will be providing most of the vitamin C needed by your family. The citrus will provide other nutrients, too.

Buying dark leafy greens and deep yellow vegetables or fruits will provide important amounts of vitamin A. These and tomatoes, cabbage, white potatoes and other fruits and vegetables also contribute vitamin C and minerals.

In many cases you choose to buy some of the fruits and vegetables your family needs from the shelves that display the product in colorfully labeled cans. At other times you may choose to get these foods from the freezer chest. In some cases you may choose them in the dried form. And, of course, if you are lucky enough to have your own garden and orchard, you'll take many fruits and vegetables from your own supply.

If you plant a garden, include a good choice of the dark green and deep yellow vegetables . . . some of these can be stored in root cellars for winter use, or you may can or freeze what you don't eat fresh. In season, your own tomatoes or fresh raw strawberries are good sources of vitamin C, for example.

You will want to buy (and/or grow) enough fruits and vegetables in one or another of these forms to provide each person with three or four servings a day. This includes the citrus fruit mentioned earlier. Fruit and vegetables will bring to your meals and snacks a variety of color, flavor and texture, all of which add enjoyment to eating.

Questions and Answers

Q. There are a lot of vegetables that are not "dark green" or "deep yellow." What about cauliflower, turnips, summer squash, onions, green beans? And what about other fruits—bananas, pears, blueberries?

A. Nutritionists always emphasize the dark green, deep yellow fruits and vegetables and the citrus fruits because they are among the best sources for two vitamins that are often in short supply in American diets . . . vitamins A and C. Once you make sure you get a vitamin C food every day, and a vitamin A food every other day, you're free to choose other fruits and vegetables for the color, flavor and interest they add to your meals. Without being excessive in calories, they also supply a good variety of nutrients—vitamins, minerals and fiber.

Q. How many vegetables should be included in a dinner menu?

A. There are no fixed rules for the kinds and amounts of foods to include in each meal. This is a matter of individual preference. Some members of your family may prefer to eat vegetables between meals, as snack foods, to accompany a sandwich.

Q. Should one cut out potatoes if on a diet?

A. Potatoes are too good a source of minerals and vitamins to ignore. If you have to watch your food budget, they're one of your nutritional bargains. It is not wise, ever, to diet by eliminating an entire food category such as potatoes, or bread. But you might examine your method of cooking potatoes. Three ounces of French fried potatoes contain about 235 calories. But there are only about 90 calories in one medium size baked potato, peeled after baking. With a pat of butter or margarine, 125 calories.

Q. How do canned and frozen vegetables compare in value with the fresh products?

A. Canned and frozen vegetables contain a high proportion of the nutrients originally present when the vegetables are handled and prepared commercially, or in the home by modern approved methods.

Q. How much loss is there when the liquid in canned vegetables is poured off?

A. Approximately one third of the minerals and vitamins present may be lost, so you may want to use that liquid in soup or gravy.

DAIRY CASE

Next, you may go to the dairy case which displays milk, cheese, yogurt, ice cream, etc. Here you will be buying your surest source of calcium. These foods also provide high quality protein, riboflavin, vitamin A and many other nutrients.

The variety here is not as great as in fruits and vegetables, but there is still plenty to choose from:

Whole milk contains about 3.5 per cent fat and this fat carries vitamin A. Much of the whole milk on the market is homogenized. Whole milk often has vitamin A and vitamin D added and its label will tell you if so, and how much.

Skim milk is whole milk that has had practically all the fat removed, taking with it the vitamin A and about half the calories. However, much of the skim milk on the market has vitamins A and D added (check the label).

"Two per cent" milk is whole milk with some of the fat removed and nonfat dry milk solids added to increase the protein content.

Buttermilk, as a rule, is skim milk with a lactic acid culture added and it has the same nutrients and calories as skim milk.

Nonfat dry milk is skim milk that has had most of the water removed. It may also have vitamins A and D added. And you will find it among the baking staples in your food store, not in the dairy case.

Evaporated milk is whole milk with about half the water removed. Do not confuse this with *canned condensed milk* which has sugar added and is used chiefly for making desserts and toppings. These canned products are located with baking staples.

Here is a guide to amounts of milk your family needs each day:

	8-ounce cups
Children under 9	2 to 3
Children 9 to 12 and pregnant women	3 or more
Teen-agers and nursing mothers	4 or more
Adults	2 or more

The next table shows you how much cheese or yogurt or other milk product it takes to provide the same amount of calcium as milk:

1 oz. Cheddar type cheese	=¾ c. milk
½ c. yogurt	=½ c. milk
½ c. cottage cheese	=⅓ c. milk
2 tblsp. cream cheese	=1 tblsp. milk
½ c. ice cream or ice milk	=⅓ c. milk

The dairy case also displays all kinds of natural cheeses and pasteurized process cheeses, cheese foods and cheese spreads.

Natural cheese is a product made by coagulating milk and then separating the curd, or solid part, from the whey, or watery part. Some natural cheeses are ripened (aged) to develop their characteristic flavor and texture; among the best-known are Cheddar, Monterey Jack, blue, Swiss, Parmesan, Romano, Muenster. Fresh (unripened) natural cheeses include cottage cheese, cream cheese, Neufchatel, ricotta and mozzarella.

Pasteurized process cheese is a blend of fresh and aged natural cheeses that have been melted, pasteurized and mixed with an emulsifier. Other ingredients, such as fruits, vegetables, meats or spices may be added. Process cheeses lose some of the characteristic flavor of natural cheeses during manufacture; also the texture becomes uniform and soft. Pasteurization prevents further ripening; therefore, the texture and flavor remain constant after processing. Process cheeses melt easily and blend well with other foods. The most popular is pasteurized process American cheese, made from natural Cheddar and similar varieties.

Pasteurized process cheese food and cheese spread contain less cheese and less fat than process cheese, but have added milk and whey solids.

Eggs, butter and margarine are also displayed in the dairy case, but from a nutritional standpoint, eggs belong in the meat group, and butter and margarine are fats, which will be mentioned later.

Questions and Answers

Q. Is it possible for a person to drink too much milk?

A. Yes, if milk is consumed in such large amounts that it crowds out other important foods in the diet. Some people, particularly young children, are lazy eaters and prefer to drink their food instead of chewing it. They are likely to fill up on milk and not have the appetite or space for the other foods they need. For them, milk should be rationed and given at the end of a meal or in a snack.

Q. Is it all right to give a young child skim milk?

A. Yes, with two "ifs": If the skim milk is fortified with vitamins A and D. And if the child has enough appetite to get the calories he needs from other foods.

Q. What is creamed cottage cheese?

A. Creamed cottage cheese is dry cottage cheese with cream or cream and milk added to improve the texture and flavor. Butterfat content must be at least 4 per cent—which adds approximately three calories per tablespoonful. It's usually available in two curd sizes, small and large. In some recipes the kind of cottage cheese and the size of the curd is specified because it can make a difference in the results.

MEAT

On to the section offering meat, poultry and fish. Here you are buying your favorite, most flavorful sources of protein—and high quality protein at that!

With this protein you are getting all the B-vitamins, important amounts of iron and several other minerals.

Most homemakers serve larger portions of meat, poultry or

fish—especially to the men—than is absolutely necessary for a nutritious diet. So do restaurants—the popular eight-ounce steak is bigger than you need. Four ounces of raw meat, fish or poultry, without bone, when cooked will make an acceptable and adequate serving. Two such servings per day are recommended—or their equivalent in the form of eggs, dried peas, dried beans, lentils and peanuts or peanut butter.

Questions and Answers

Q. My husband is trying to lose weight, and he insists he can eat all the meat he wants because it is a low-calorie food.

A. Many people cherish a mistaken idea that protein is low in calories while carbohydrates are high-calorie foods. One gram of either of them yields four calories. Contrast this with fat: one gram of fat yields nine calories. About two thirds of the calories in a nicely-marbled sirloin steak, for instance, come from its fat.

Your husband needs to eat lean meats. And he also needs to pay attention to the size of servings. Reducing the size of servings not only lowers calories but it also gives other foods a place in the meal.

Neither you nor your husband should make the mistake of relating carbohydrates principally to calories. On the broad spectrum, carbohydrates—well selected and in customary use—provide an assortment of important nutrients.

Q. Is expensive meat, like steak, more nutritious than less-expensive cuts like stew beef?

A. No. The difference in price reflects difference in texture and tenderness. A less-expensive cut may have slightly more protein and less fat than the well-marbled steak with its edge of fat.

Q. No one in my family likes liver or organ meats. How important are they?

A. Liver is an excellent source of protein and most vitamins and minerals, but it isn't necessary to eat liver to get these. A varied, adequate diet will supply them.

Q. Can vegetable protein be substituted equally for animal protein?

A. Vegetable proteins generally fail to provide the complete assortment of amino acids (building blocks of protein) in the amounts the body needs for growth and operation.

Q. But aren't soybeans a high quality protein food?

A. Proteins from legumes, especially soybeans, chickpeas and peanuts, are almost as good as proteins from animal sources. Soybeans are the major source for "textured vegetable protein" which you may be familiar with as meat extenders and "meatless meats."

Soy protein contains all eight amino acids which are essential for human needs. However, it is more effectively used by the body when the content of one of the amino acids, methionine, is increased. To achieve this, protein from other sources such as wheat, corn, milk and egg white may be added. Thus, meat extenders can have the same protein efficiency ratings as meat products.

Q. Do Americans eat enough protein?

A. Protein is not likely to be in short supply in American diets. Most Americans are meat eaters and we tend to eat larger portions than are needed to satisfy the RDA for protein and other nutrients.

Protein deficiency is a major problem in many parts of the world and is one reason for research now going on to develop more palatable soybean products and grains with higher protein quality, such as high lysine corn.

Q. Do eggs contain as much iron as meat?

A. Yes. Equal quantities by weight of eggs and the lean part of meat contribute about the same amount of iron.

Q. Why are eggs necessary in the diet?

A. No single food is essential. It is the nutrients that are essential and they are found in many foods. Eggs are valuable because they're a good and convenient source of high-quality protein, iron and vitamin A.

Q. Must every meal include meat, fish, poultry or eggs?

A. No, but the body uses protein more effectively when some animal protein is included in each meal. Milk products are just as effective as meats, etc.

BREAD, FLOUR AND CEREALS

As you check the selections in your shopping cart, you will be aware that you have not yet bought any breads, flour or cereals . . . so helpful and, in fact, so necessary to the assembling of most meals and snacks.

Derived from grains, food in this group furnishes worthwhile amounts of protein, trace minerals and several vitamins, especially the B-vitamins. No doubt you are most familiar with products that appear as *whole grain* or as *refined*.

The whole grain contains the outer bran layer of the original cereal, plus the inner germ, plus the endosperm or starchy kernel.

Refined products, such as all-purpose flour, farina and some prepared breakfast cereals, have had the bran and germ removed by extensive milling. Such milling removes the valuable nutrients in the bran and germ. To partly compensate for this loss, many refined flours and cereals, including macaroni products, corn meal and rice, are *enriched* by adding three of the B-vitamins (thiamin, niacin and riboflavin) and iron. Even so, enrichment does not restore all the nutrients lost in milling.

However, milling wheat produces a fine white flour suitable for home baking. Removing the bran and germ makes the flour more stable, so that it can be stored for long periods. That is why wheat was milled to white flour in the first place.

Whole grain flour and wheat germ are ingredients in many of the bread recipes in this book. Because they are perishable, buy small quantities and store them in the refrigerator or freezer.

Many breakfast cereals are labeled "fortified." This means that substantial amounts of vitamins and minerals have been added so that the product supplies much more than the original grain or grains from which it is made. The kind and amounts of the different nutrients in the product are given on the label.

At least four servings a day from this group of foods are usually recommended.

Questions and Answers

Q. What is wheat germ?

A. Wheat germ is the portion of the kernel called the embryo, from which the new plant starts its growth. It is about 2 or 3 per cent of the kernel. The germ is a concentrated source of protein, iron, vitamin E and the B-vitamins. Its nutritional contribution to the ordinary diet is limited however, because of the small amounts generally eaten, alone or combined with other foods.

Q. I always thought bran was important mainly for the fiber it adds to the diet. Does bran also furnish nutrients?

A. Yes. In addition to indigestible cellulose material (fiber or roughage), bran contains 19 per cent of the protein in the wheat kernel, plus important amounts of the B-vitamins.

Q. The labels on some ready-to-eat breakfast foods say that one serving supplies 100 per cent of the U.S. RDA for several vitamins and iron. Is this an acceptable way to get the vitamins you need each day?

A. There is no evidence that the body can use a whole day's supply at one time. Considering the interdependence of the nutrients (how they work together to perform services for the body), and considering the fact that the body cannot store some of these nutrients, it seems unlikely that a one-shot dose of vitamins every twenty-four hours, whether in cereal or capsule form, would be as efficient as getting them in various food combinations throughout the day.

Q. Are sugar-coated cereals bad for children?

A. It depends on the total day's diet. Few children (or adults) will eat cereal without some sweetening. However, you should be reading labels. The chief ingredient in any food product must be listed first on its label. You may be surprised to find some cereal boxes listing sugar first or second. This means that the nutritive contribution of the cereal has been seriously diluted.

SUGAR

Besides flour, another staple is sugar, an ingredient not only in many of your recipes, but also a component of many processed or packaged foods. Most Americans get more sugar than they need—or realize.

Sugar and syrups are valuable from the standpoint of adding flavor to other foods and in counteracting tartness, especially in fruits. Sugar is essential in giving desirable texture and flavor to baked goods. It is a good preservative in jams and jellies.

Sugar also supplies energy, but unlike most other foods, there are no other nutrients riding along. Too many sweets can satisfy the appetite and can crowd out other types of foods which you need for good nutrition, and also can contribute to tooth decay.

Questions and Answers

Q. Are honey and syrup "natural foods?" Are they healthier than sugar? And what about brown sugar?

A. Honey is about three fourths sugar, the rest water. Molasses, sorghum and dark brown sugar furnish some iron and calcium, but their chief value is the energy or calories they contribute—and their good taste.

Q. What is raw sugar?

A. Raw sugar is the unrefined residue after the removal of molasses from cane juice. It contains a fairly high proportion of some minerals, but like refined sugar, is mainly carbohydrate.

Q. Does jam add nutrients to the diet?

A. Jam is principally a carbohydrate food, and it is a concentrated source of calories. It contains small amounts of minerals and vitamins. In the quantities usually eaten, the nutrients contributed are not significant in the diet.

Q. Dentists are always emphasizing the relationship between sugar or candy and children's tooth decay. What can I, a mother of three small children, do about the problem?

A. While your children are still forming their taste preferences, introduce them to healthy, appetizing foods in both snacks and meals, so they acquire a liking for them. Fruits, for instance. When you sweeten food, do it sparingly. Sweeten only the foods that really need it. Don't let the kids develop a "sweet tooth," or learn to like excessively sweet food. And try to establish the habit of brushing teeth soon after eating sweets. Adults would be smart to do the same.

FATS AND OILS

Fats and oils are the most concentrated source of food energy, the chief sources of necessary fatty acids, and they may carry some fat soluble vitamins, too.

Everyone needs some fat in his diet; not only for energy and nutrients, but also to feel "satisfied." A diet too restricted in fat is bulky because a greater volume of food is needed to satisfy the appetite and meet energy needs.

But it is easy to eat too much fat, because it is used so liberally to enhance the flavor and texture of foods. Much of the fat we eat is "invisible" because it is part of the composition of foods, such as milk, cheese, meat, desserts and many baked goods. It is there but we don't see it as we do when we spread butter or margarine on a slice of bread.

There is no standard recommendation for the amount of fats and oils you need each day. Generally, you are urged to cut down on your fat intake.

However, it is important that some of the fat you get each day come from vegetable oils that supply polyunsaturated fatty acids, especially linoleic acid.

Questions and Answers

Q. Why is vegetable oil so important?

A. Certain vegetable oils are the best sources of the polyunsaturated fatty acid, linoleic acid. This is essential to life itself, and must be supplied by food because the body cannot make it. Also, some studies show that a good intake of polyunsaturated oils helps to lower the cholesterol level in the blood. An undesirably high level of cholesterol is one of the risk factors associated with coronary heart disease.

Q. Saturated, unsaturated, polyunsaturated—what do they all mean?

A. *Saturated* means that the fatty acids are saturated with all the hydrogen they can hold. Saturated fats are usually solid at room temperature. They occur chiefly in animal fats— meats and dairy products.

Unsaturated fatty acids contain less hydrogen. And of these, the *polyunsaturated* fatty acids have the least hydrogen. Linoleic acid is the most common polyunsaturated fatty acid. Or, to put it another way, a polyunsaturated fat is one with a high percentage of linoleic acid.

Polyunsaturated fats are usually oils and are most abundant in plant seeds. Best sources are safflower, sunflower, corn, cottonseed and soybean oils, and the oil in walnuts.

Nearly all fats from plant sources are unsaturated; the only major exception is coconut oil, which is highly saturated. Olive oil and peanut oil are considerably lower than the others in linoleic acid.

Q. Are vegetable shortenings and margarines saturated or unsaturated?

A. To make solid shortenings and margarine, vegetable oils are partially hardened by adding hydrogen to them. This process is called hydrogenation. Depending on the formula, the product usually is a blend of vegetable oil, some of which is "partially hydrogenated."

Q. How can I tell which product to buy to get the essential fatty acids?

A. Read the label. Ingredients have to be listed in descending order according to their presence in the product. If one of the polyunsaturated oils listed above appears at the top of the ingredient list on a tub or stick of margarine, for example, it will supply more of the essential fatty acids than a product listing "partially hardened" or "partially hydrogenated" oil first.

Q. How much polyunsaturated oil should I feed my family every day?

A. It is suggested that about one third of the total fat intake (including the "invisible" fat in foods) should come from polyunsaturated oils. This is not hard to achieve if you use table spreads and salad oils that are good sources of the polyunsaturated fatty acids.

CONVENIENCE FOODS

You may choose to buy some of the foods for your family in the form of "convenience foods" . . . those that are partially or completely ready to eat. Sometimes we refer to such foods as having "built-in maid service," because they are time and energy savers for the homemaker. Such maid service may be as simple as having carrots with tops already cut off, or bread cut into slices. Or it could be as extensive as a complete dinner of meat, potato and two vegetables—all prepared, arranged on a tray and frozen, ready to heat and eat.

The important thing in considering convenience foods is not to confuse the cost of saving time and labor with the cost of the nutritive value of the food. It is not unusual for a homemaker to complain about the high cost of nutritious meals and snacks, when actually she is spending a sizeable proportion of her food money for *services,* and for *packaging* and, in the case of frozen foods, for the zero-cold *storage* to keep the food frozen until she buys it. She does this to save herself work when she gets the food into her kitchen. How much you can afford to spend to save yourself time and labor depends on how much money you have to spend on food, and how you want or need to use your time.

INDEX

Amino Acids, 177, 189

Appetizers, *see* Beverages, Dips,
    Soups

Apples(s)
    Cake Dessert, 161
    Caramel Chocolate Apples, 19
    Cranberry Pitcher Punch, 44
    Honey Fruit Bread, 81
    Torte, 99
    Wintertime Minted Fruit Cup,
      37

Applesauce
    Cake, 151
    Oatmeal Drops, 149
    Swedish Apple Pudding, 160

Apricot(s)
    Dessert, Diet, 37
    Good Health Bars, 147
    Logs, Golden, 18
    Prune Pie, Pioneer, 157

Banana(s)
    Chocolate Shake, 96
    Cookies, 143
    Custards, High-Hat, 97
    High Nutrition Cake, 155
    Nut Bread, 83
    Popsicles, 36
    Three Fruit Sherbet, 35
    Wintertime Minted Fruit Cup,
      37

Barbecued Meatball Sandwich, 116

Basic Hamburger Patties, 117

Bean(s), *see also* Green beans,
    Kidney beans
    Baked Bean Salad, 57
    Mexican Bean Salad, 57
    Ready-to-Pour Bean Soup, 49
    Stuffed Frankfurters, 123

Beef
    Barbecued Meatball Sandwich,
      116
    Basic Hamburger Patties, 117
    Bran Meat Loaf, 120
    Burger Dogs, 122
    Dip, Zippy, 102
    Ground Beef Mini-Meal, 132
    Hamburger Pizzas, 127
    Italian Meatball Sandwich, 116
    Italian Vegetable Soup, 129
    Mexican Cheeseburgers, 107
    Oven-Freezer Meatballs, 115
    Slim Jim Cheeseburger, 33
    Sloppy Joe Barbecue
      Sandwiches, 121
    Snackers' Casseroles, 131
    Taco Fillings, 125
    Texas Vegetable Soup, 130
    Vegetable Soup, 28

Beets
    Chilled Borscht, 49
    Low-Cal Borscht, 27

Beverages
  Apple Cranberry Pitcher Punch, 44
  Chocolate Banana Shake, 96
  Chocolate Peppermint Shake, 96
  Double Chocolate Shake, 97
  Friendship Punch, 45
  Frosty Orange Nog, 46
  Garden Tomato Juice, 47–48
  Golden Grape Punch, 44
  Grape Frost, 95
  Homemade Ice Cream Soda, 93
  Mexican Chocolate, 95
  Mulled Tomato Juice, 23
  Old-Fashioned Eggnog, 94
  Orange Cider Punch, 45
  Orange Slush, 94
  Pink Frost, 43
  Pitcher Grape Punch, 44
  Strawberry Fizz, 24
  Super Strawberry Malt, 94
  Tropical Fruit Shake, 43
  Vanilla Milk Shake, 96
Blueberry Sicles, 34
Blue Cheese
  Onions, 50
  Tomatoes, 51
Bologna Cheesewiches, 114
Borscht
  Chilled, 49
  Low-Cal, 27
Bran, 191
  Banana Nut Bread, 83
  Fruited Bran Cookies, 146
  Meat Loaf, 120
  Prune Bran Bread, 72
  Raisin Muffins, 85
  Surprise Cloverleafs, 78
  Whole Wheat Bran Bread, 70
Braunschweiger Dip, 120
Bread, see also Muffins, Rolls
  Banana Nut, 83
  Easy Oatmeal, 74
  Four-Grain, 66

  High Protein White, 71
  Honey Fruit, 81
  Mixed Grain Raisin, 65
  nutrients in, 190–91
  Pecan Bran, 72
  Pumpkin Raisin Loaf, 82
  Wheat Batter, 73
  Whole Wheat, 67
  Whole Wheat Bran, 70
  Whole Wheat Buttermilk, 68
  Whole Wheat Protein, 69
  Zucchini Nut, 84
Breakfast cereals, 191–92
Broccoli
  Marinated Vegetables, 58
  Salad, 32
Burger Dogs, 122
Buttermilk, 185
  Strawberry Sherbet, 35
  Whole Wheat Bread, 68
Butterscotch Pumpkin Pudding, 38
B-vitamins, 187, 190, 191

Cabbage
  Mediterranean Salad, 32
  Vegetable Slaw, 31
Cake
  Apple Cake Dessert, 161
  Applesauce, 151
  Cranberry Calico, 150
  High Nutrition, 155
  Oatmeal, 154
  Orange Sponge, 152
  Spicy Lemon Prune, 153
  Strawberry Angel Dessert, 98
Calcium, 177, 184, 186
Calories
  daily needs, 1–2
  in meat, 188
  in milk, 93, 185
Candy, see Confections
Caramel Chocolate Apples, 19
Carbohydrates, 188

Carrots
  Confetti Sauerkraut Salad, 56
  Italian Vegetable Soup, 129
  Marinated Vegetables, 58
  Oatmeal Raisin Cookies, 144
  Orange and Yellow Salad, 59
  Refrigerator Carrot Salad, 53
  Slaw, 54
Cashew-Date Drops, 142
Casserole(s)
  Date Cookies, 18
  Ground Beef Mini-Meal, 132
  Individual Chicken, 134
  Snackers', 131
  Tuna Vegetable, 133
Cauliflower
  Marinated Vegetables, 58
  Parmesan Garden Salad Bowl,
    56
Caviar, Poor Man's, 48
Celery
  Dilly Cheese-Stuffed, 24
  Pineapple Cheese-Stuffed, 25
Cereal, breakfast, 190–92
Cereal Snacks
  Cereal Snack Mix, 10
  Corn Nut Toffee, 16
  Country-Style Granola, 13
  Date Coconut Balls, 17
  Peanut Cereal Bar Cookies, 17
  Peanut Cereal Snack Mix, 12
  Peanut Cocoa-Cereal Bars, 16
  Popcorn Cereal Crunch, 11
Cheese, 186. See also Cottage
    Cheese
  Bologna Cheesewiches, 114
  Cheese Potato Salad, 107
  Cheesy Fishburger, 105
  Dilled Cheese Dip, 100
  Dilly Cheese-Stuffed Celery, 24
  Easy Nachos, 104
  Grilled Tortilla Sandwiches, 105
  Ham and Cheese Muffins, 106
  Hamburger Pizzas, 127
  Italian Chef's Salad Mix, 55
  Liverwurst Reubens, 112
  Luncheon Meat Cheese
    Sandwiches, 114
  Mexican Cheeseburgers, 107
  Parmesan Tuna Dip, 102
  Peachy Cheese Dessert, 35
  Pineapple Cheese Dip, 100
  Pineapple Cheese-Stuffed Celery,
    24
  Pineapple Cheese Pie, 158
  Pizza Muffins, 117
  Potted Cheese, 101
  Reuben Sandwich Filling, 112
  Sausage Pizzas, 127
  Slim Jim Cheeseburger, 33
  Snackers' Casseroles, 131
  Stuffed Frankfurters, 123
  Swiss Salmon Sandwiches, 118
  Tacos, 125
  Tuna Buns, 124
  Zesty Cheese Dip, 26
Cheesy Fishburger, 105
Chicken
  Casseroles, Individual, 134
  Vegetable Soup, 128
Chilled Borscht, 49
Chocolate
  Banana Shake, 96
  Caramel Apples, 19
  Chip Cookies, Super, 141
  Mexican, 95
  Peanut Spread, 162
  Peppermint Shake, 96
Cider Punch, Orange, 45
Cinnamon
  Pear Muffins, 86
  Whole Wheat Rolls, 76
Clam Dip, Low-Cal, 25
Cocoa-Cereal Peanut Bars, 16
Coconut
  Casserole Date Cookies, 18
  Country-Style Granola, 13
  Date Balls, 17

Five-Cup Snack Mix, 13
Fruited Bran Cookies, 146
Fruit Nut Balls, 15
Golden Apricot Logs, 18
Oatmeal Fruit Cookies, 146
Confectioners Sugar Icing, 76
Confections
  Caramel Chocolate Apples, 19
  Date Coconut Balls, 17
  Golden Apricot Logs, 18
  Peanut-Date Balls, 148
Confetti Sauerkraut Salad, 56
Cookies
  Applesauce Oatmeal Drops, 149
  Banana, 143
  Cashew-Date Drops, 142
  Casserole Date Cookies, 18
  Fruitcake Squares, 148
  Fruited Bran, 146
  Good Health Bars, 147
  Granola, 143
  Honeyed Raisin, 141
  Molasses Ginger, 145
  Oatmeal Fruit, 146
  Peanut Cereal Bar, 17
  Peanut Cocoa-Cereal Bars, 16
  Pea-Nutty, 140
  Raisin Carrot Oatmeal, 144
  Sunflower Refrigerator Cookies,
    139
  Super Chocolate Chip, 141
Corn
  Mixed Vegetable Salad, 59
  Nut Toffee, 16
  Orange and Yellow Salad, 59
  Succotash Salad, 53
  Texas Vegetable Soup, 130
Corned Beef
  Reuben Sandwich Filling, 112
Cottage Cheese, 186, 187
  Dilly Cheese-Stuffed Celery, 24
  filling for pie, 158
  French Onion Dip, 25
  Low-Cal Clam Dip, 25

Muffins, 87
Peachy Cheese Dessert, 35
Sandwiches, 104
Slimmers' Deviled Eggs, 27
Tuna Salad Sandwiches, 34
Zesty Cheese Dip, 26
Zippy Beef Dip, 102
Country-Style Granola, 13
Cranberry(ies), Cranberry Juice
  Calico Cake, 150
  Friendship Punch, 21
  Orange Sherbet, 38
  Pink Frost, 43
  Pitcher Punch, 44
Cream cheese, 186, 187
  Frosting, 152
  Glaze, Lemon, 154
  -Tuna Spread, 103
Cucumber
  Dilled Pineapple-Cucumber
    Salad, 60
  Mediterranean Salad, 32
  Yogurt Soup, 30
Custard, Maple, 98
Custard Sauce, 161

Dairy foods, 91–93, 184–87
Dates
  Apple Torte, 99
  Cashew-Date Drops, 142
  Casserole Date Cookies, 18
  Coconut Balls, 17
  Cranberry Calico Cake, 150
  Fruitcake Squares, 148
  Fruited Bran Cookies, 146
  Fruit Nut Balls, 15
  Honey Fruit Bread, 81
  Oatmeal Crescents, 79
  Oatmeal Fruit Cookies, 146
  Peanut Date Balls, 148
  Super Fruited Muffins, 85
Denver Sandwich, Easy, 122
Desserts, 137–62. See also Cakes,
    Cookies, Pies

Apple Cake Dessert, 161
Apple Torte, 99
Blueberry Sicles, 34
Butterscotch Pumpkin Pudding, 38
Cranberry Orange Sherbet, 38
Diet Apricot, 37
Fruit-Yogurt Combo, 61
High-Hat Banana Custards, 97
Maple Custard, 98
Peaches with Spicy Yogurt, 37
Peachy Cheese Dessert, 35
Strawberry Angel Dessert, 98
Strawberry Buttermilk Sherbet, 35
Swedish Apple Pudding, 160
Wintertime Minted Fruit Cup, 37
Deviled Eggs, Slimmers', 27
Diet Apricot Dessert, 37
Dilled
  Cheese Dip, 100
  Dilly Cheese-Stuffed Celery, 24
  Green Beans, 30
  Pineapple-Cucumber Salad, 60
Dips
  Braunschweiger, 120
  Dilled Cheese, 100
  French Onion, 25
  Low-Cal Clam, 25
  Parmesan Tuna, 102
  Pineapple Cheese, 100
  Poor Man's Caviar, 48
  Strawberry, 97
  Tuna Butter, 119
  Zesty Cheese, 26
  Zippy Beef, 102
Double Chocolate Shake, 97
Double Peanut Popcorn Balls, 15

Easy Denver Sandwich, 122
Easy Nachos, 104
Easy Oatmeal Bread, 74

Eggs
  Broccoli Salad, 32
  Easy Denver Sandwich, 122
  Egg Salad Sandwiches, 33
  Freezer French Toast, 88
  nutrients in, 189–90
  Old-Fashioned Eggnog, 94
  Scandinavian Egg Salad, 119
  Slimmers' Deviled Eggs, 27
Eggplant
  Poor Man's Caviar, 48
English Oat Muffins, 80

Fats, 193–95
  in meat, 188
  in milk, 185
Fatty acids, 177, 193–95
Fiber, in foods, 4, 191
Fillings
  Cottage Cheese, 158
  Date-Nut, 79
  Raisin Nut, 78
Fish, 188
Fishburger, Cheesy, 105
Five-Cup Snack Mix, 13
Flour, 64, 190–91
Four-Grain Bread, 66
Frankfurters, Stuffed, 123
Freezer French Toast, 88
French Onion Dip, 25
French Toast, Freezer, 88
Friendship Punch, 45
Frosting
  Confectioners Sugar Icing, 76
  Cream Cheese, 152
Frosty Orange Nog, 46
Frozen Wheat Waffles, 89
Fruit, see also Individual Fruits
  Fruitcake Squares, 148
  Fruited Bran Cookies, 146
  Fruit Nut Balls, 15
  Fruit-Yogurt Combo, 61
  Honey Fruit Bread, 81
  nutrients in fruits, 7–8, 182–83

Oatmeal Fruit Cookies, 146
Super Fruited Muffins, 85
Three Fruit Sherbet, 35
Tropical Fruit Shake, 43
Wintertime Minted Fruit Cup, 37

Garden Tomato Juice, 47
Gazpacho, 28
Ginger Cookies, Molasses, 145
Glaze
    Lemon Cheese, 154
    Orange, 151
Golden Apricot Logs, 18
Golden Grape Punch, 44
Golden Tartar Sauce, 106
Good Health Bars, 147
Graham Crackers
    Crust, 158
    Swedish Apple Pudding, 160
Granola Cookies, 143
Granola, Country-Style, 13
Grapes, Grape Juice
    Fruit-Yogurt Combo, 61
    Golden Grape Punch, 44
    Grape Frost, 95
    Pitcher Grape Punch, 44
Green Beans
    Dilled Green Beans, 30
    Italian Potato Salad, 54
    Italian Vegetable Soup, 129
    Mixed Vegetable Salad, 59
    Succotash Salad, 53
Green Pepper
    Cabbage Vegetable Slaw, 31
    Confetti Sauerkraut Salad, 56
    Italian Chef's Salad Mix, 55
    Mixed Vegetable Relish, 60
    Orange and Yellow Salad, 59
Grilled Tortilla Sandwiches, 105
Ground Beef
    Barbecued Meatball Sandwich, 116
    Basic Hamburger Patties, 117

Beef Vegetable Soup, 28
Bran Meat Loaf, 120
Burger Dogs, 122
Hamburger Pizzas, 127
Italian Meatball Sandwich, 116
Mexican Cheeseburgers, 107
Mini-Meal, 132
Oven-Freezer Meatballs, 115
Slim Jim Cheeseburgers, 33
Sloppy Joe Barbecue
    Sandwiches, 121
Snackers' Casseroles, 131
Taco filling, 125
Texas Vegetable Soup, 130

Ham
    and Cheese Muffins, 106
    Italian Chef's Salad Mix, 55
Hamburger Pizzas, 127
High-Hat Banana Custards, 97
High Nutrition Cake, 155
High Protein White Bread, 71
Homemade Ice Cream Soda, 93
Homemade Pizza Sauce, 126
Honey, 192
    Fruit Bread, 81
    Honeyed Raisin Cookies, 141
    Nut Butter, 14
Hydrogenation of vegetable oils, 194–95

Ice Cream, see also Ice Milk
    Apple Torte, 99
    calcium supplied by, 186
    Chocolate Banana Shake, 96
    Chocolate Peppermint Shake, 96
    Double Chocolate Shake, 97
    Frosty Orange Nog, 46
    Grape Frost, 95
    Homemade Ice Cream Soda, 93
    Orange Pops, 47
    Orange Slush, 94
    Pink Frost, 43
    Pioneer Apricot Prune Pie, 157

Super Strawberry Malt, 94
Tropical Fruit Shake, 43
Vanilla Milk Shake, 96
Ice Milk
Diet Apricot Dessert, 37
Icing
Confectioners Sugar, 76
Individual Chicken Casseroles, 134
Individual Pizza Crusts, 126
Iron, 178
in breakfast cereals, 191–92
in eggs, 190
in flour, 190
in meat, 187
in wheat germ, 191
Italian
Chef's Salad Mix, 55
Meatball Sandwich, 116
Potato Salad, 54
-Style Sloppy Joes, 118
Vegetable Soup, 129

Kidney Beans
Italian Chef's Salad Mix, 55
Italian Vegetable Soup, 129
Mexican Bean Salad, 57
Mixed Vegetable Salad, 59
Texas Vegetable Soup, 130

Legumes, 189
Lemon
Cheese Glaze, 154
Fluff Pie, 159
Prune Cake, Spicy, 153
Lentils, 188
Linoleic acid, 194
Liver, 188–89
Braunschweiger Dip, 120
Liverwurst Reubens, 112
Low-Cal Borscht, 27
Low-Cal Clam Dip, 25
Low-Calorie Snacks, 21–39
Luncheon Meat Cheese
Sandwiches, 114

Maple Custard, 98
Margarines, 195
Marinated
Sausage Sandwiches, 113
Tomatoes, 51
Vegetables, 58
Meal Planning, see also Menus
eating patterns in U.S., 1–4
incorporating snacks, 3
meats, 188
milk requirements, 185
need for variety, 4, 8, 178
what size snacks, 7
when to snack, 6–7
Meat, see also Beef, Ground Beef,
Sausage
Barbecued Meatball Sandwich,
116
Bran Meat Loaf, 120
Italian Meatball Sandwich, 116
Italian-Style Sloppy Joes, 118
Luncheon Meat Cheese
Sandwiches, 114
meatless meats, 189
nutrients in meat, 187–90
Oven-Freezer Meatballs, 115
Stuffed Frankfurters, 123
Mediterranean Salad, 32
Menus, 168–76
Mexican
Bean Salad, 57
Cheeseburgers, 107
Chocolate, 95
Milk and milk products, 91–108
nutritional information about,
184–87
Milk Drinks, 93–97
Minerals, 3, 7, 8, 177, 178, 190
Mixed Grain Raisin Bread, 65
Mixed Vegetable Relish, 60
Mixed Vegetable Salad, 59
Molasses, 192
Molasses Ginger Cookies, 145
Muffins

Bran Raisin, 85
Cinnamon Pear, 86
Cottage Cheese, 87
English Oat, 80
Super Fruited, 85
Mulled Tomato Juice, 23

Nachos, Easy, 104
New-Fashioned Pumpkin Pie, 157
Nonfat dry milk, 185
Nutrient density in foods, 7
Nutrients, 177–78
  in fruit and vegetable snacks, 41–43
  in meat cuts, 188
  in milk and milk products, 91–92
  in nibbles or finger foods, 9–10
  interdependence of, 177
Nutrition
  eating patterns in U.S., 1–4
  healthier snacking, 2–8, 165–68
  milk equivalents, 185–86
  need for variety in diet, 4, 8, 178
  nutrients vs. calories, 7
  nutrition labeling, 179–81
  sources of information on, 178
Nut(s), *see also* Peanuts
  Apple Torte, 99
  Banana Cookies, 143
  Banana Nut Bread, 83
  Cashew-Date Drops, 142
  Casserole Date Cookies, 18
  Corn Nut Toffee, 16
  Date Coconut Balls, 17
  Date Oatmeal Crescents, 79
  Five-Cup Snack Mix, 13
  Fruitcake Squares, 148
  Fruited Bran Cookies, 146
  Fruit Nut Balls, 15
  Oatmeal Cake, 154
  Oatmeal Fruit Cookies, 146
  Peppy Popcorn, 12

Popcorn Cereal Crunch, 11
Pumpkin Raisin Loaf, 82
Spicy, 14
Spicy Lemon Prune Cake, 153
Surprise Cloverleafs, 78
Zucchini Nut Bread, 84

Oatmeal
  Applesauce Oatmeal Drops, 149
  Cake, 154
  Date Crescents, 79
  Easy Oatmeal Bread, 74
  English Oat Muffins, 80
  Four-Grain Bread, 66
  Fruit Cookies, 146
  Raisin Carrot Cookies, 144
  Sunflower Refrigerator Cookies, 139
Oils, 193–95
Old-Fashioned Eggnog, 94
Onions
  Blue Cheese, 50
  French Onion Dip, 25
Orange and Yellow Salad, 59
Orange(s), Orange Juice
  Banana Popsicles, 36
  Cider Punch, 45
  Cranberry Orange Sherbet, 38
  Frosty Orange Nog, 46
  Fruit-Yogurt Combo, 61
  Glaze, 151
  Golden Grape Punch, 44
  Ice Cream Pops, 47
  nutrients in, 7, 42
  Pink Frost, 43
  Pops, 46
  Slush, 94
  Sponge Cake, 152
  Three Fruit Sherbet, 35
  Tropical Fruit Shake, 43
  Wintertime Minted Fruit Cup, 37
Oven-Freezer Meatballs, 115

Parmesan Garden Salad Bowl, 56
Parmesan Tuna Dip, 102
Party Tuna Spread, 103
Peaches with Spicy Yogurt, 37
Peachy Cheese Dessert, 35
Peanut(s), 188, 189
  Caramel Chocolate Apples, 19
  Cereal Bar Cookies, 17
  Cereal Snack Mix, 10
  Chocolate Peanut Spread, 162
  Cocoa-Cereal Bars, 16
  Country-Style Granola, 13
  -Date Balls, 148
  Double Peanut Popcorn Balls, 15
  Five-Cup Snack Mix, 13
  Granola Cookies, 143
  High Nutrition Cake, 155
  Honey Nut Butter, 14
  Oil, 195
  Pea-Nutty Cookies, 140
  Spicy Nuts, 14
Pear Cinnamon Muffins, 86
Pecan
  Sweet Potato Pie, 156
  Whole Wheat Rolls, 77
Peppermint Chocolate Shake, 96
Peppy Popcorn, 12
Pie
  Crust, Graham Cracker, 158
  Lemon Fluff, 159
  Pineapple Cheese, 158
  Pioneer Apricot Prune, 157
  Sweet Potato Pecan, 156
Pineapple, Pineapple Juice
  Cheese Dip, 100
  Cheese Pie, 158
  Cheese-Stuffed Celery, 25
  Cucumber Salad, Dilled, 60
  Friendship Punch, 45
  Fruit-Yogurt Combo, 61
  Strawberry Fizz, 24
  Three Fruit Sherbet, 35
  Topping, 159

Wintertime Minted Fruit Cup, 37
Pink Frost, 43
Pioneer Apricot Prune Pie, 157
Pitcher Grape Punch, 44
Pizzas
  Hamburger, 127
  Individual Crusts, 126
  Muffins, 117
  Sauce, Homemade, 126
  Sausage, 127
Polyunsaturated fats, 194–95
Poor Man's Caviar, 48
Popcorn
  Cereal Crunch, 11
  Double Peanut Popcorn Balls, 15
  Peppy Popcorn, 12
Popsicles
  Banana, 36
  Orange, 46
  Orange-Ice Cream Pops, 47
  Raspberry Pops, 36
Potato(es)
  Cheese Potato Salad, 107
  Chilled Borscht, 49
  Italian Potato Salad, 54
  Snackers' Casseroles, 131
Potted Cheese, 101
Poultry, 187–88
Protein
  in cereal grains, 191
  in meat and meat substitutes, 187–90
  in milk, 184–85
  U.S. consumption of, 189–90
Prune(s)
  Bran Bread, 72
  Fruit Nut Balls, 15
  Pioneer Apricot Prune Pie, 157
  Spicy Lemon Prune Cake, 153
Pudding
  Butterscotch Pumpkin, 38
  Swedish Apple, 160

Pumpkin
  Butterscotch Pudding, 38
  Pie, New-Fashioned, 157
  Raisin Loaf, 82
Punch
  Apple Cranberry Pitcher Punch, 44
  Friendship, 45
  Golden Grape Punch, 44
  Orange Cider Punch, 45
  Pitcher Grape Punch, 44

Quick Breads
  Banana Nut Bread, 83
  Bran Raisin Muffins, 85
  Cinnamon Pear Muffins, 86
  Cottage Cheese Muffins, 87
  Frozen Wheat Waffles, 89
  Honey Fruit Bread, 81
  Pumpkin Raisin Loaf, 82
  Sunflower Wheat Muffins, 87
  Super Fruited Muffins, 85
  Zucchini Nut Bread, 84

Raisins
  Applesauce Cake, 151
  Applesauce Oatmeal Drops, 149
  Apple Torte, 99
  Bran Raisin Muffins, 85
  Carrot Oatmeal Cookies, 144
  Carrot Slaw, 54
  Five-Cup Snack Mix, 13
  Fruitcake Squares, 148
  Fruited Bran Cookies, 146
  Fruit Nut Balls, 15
  Good Health Bars, 147
  Granola Cookies, 143
  Honeyed Raisin Cookies, 141
  Mixed Grain Raisin Bread, 65
  -Nut Filling, 78
  Oatmeal Fruit Cookies, 146
  Pumpkin Raisin Loaf, 82
  Surprise Cloverleafs, 78
Raspberry Pops, 36

RDA (U. S. Recommended Daily Allowance), 179, 181
Ready-to-Pour Bean Soup, 49
Refrigerator Carrot Salad, 53
Relish, Mixed Vegetable, 60
Reuben Sandwich Filling, 112
Riboflavin, 178
  in milk, 184
Rice, 190
Rolls
  Date Oatmeal Crescents, 79
  Surprise Cloverleafs, 87
  Whole Wheat Buns, 74
  Whole Wheat Cinnamon Rolls, 76
  Whole Wheat Pecan Rolls, 77
  Whole Wheat Sweet Roll Dough, 75

Salads
  Baked Bean, 57
  Blue Cheese Onions, 50
  Blue Cheese Tomatoes, 51
  Broccoli, 32
  Cabbage Vegetable Slaw, 31
  Carrot Slaw, 54
  Cheese Potato, 107
  Confetti Sauerkraut, 56
  Dilled Pineapple Cucumber, 60
  Fruit-Yogurt Combo, 61
  Italian Chef's Salad Mix, 55
  Italian Potato, 54
  Marinated Tomatoes, 51
  Marinated Vegetables, 58
  Mediterranean, 32
  Mexican Bean, 57
  Mixed Vegetable Relish, 60
  Parmesan Garden Salad Bowl, 56
  Refrigerator Carrot, 53
  Salsa, 52
  Succotash, 53
  Vegetable Marinade, 52
  Vegetable Slaw, 31

Salmon Sandwiches, Swiss, 118
Salsa, 52
Sandwiches
  Barbecued Meatball, 116
  Basic Hamburger Patties, 117
  Bologna Cheesewiches, 114
  Burger Dogs, 122
  Cheesy Fishburger, 105
  Cottage Cheese, 104
  Easy Denver, 122
  Egg Salad, 33
  Grilled Tortilla, 105
  Ham and Cheese Muffins, 106
  Hamburger Pizzas, 127
  Italian Meatball, 116
  Italian Style Sloppy Joes, 118
  Luncheon Meat Cheese, 114
  Marinated Sausage, 113
  Mexican Cheeseburgers, 107
  Pizza Muffins, 117
  Reuben Sandwich Filling, 112
  Sausage Pizzas, 127
  Scandinavian Egg Salad, 119
  Second-Time Sandwich, 111
  Slim Jim Cheeseburger, 33
  Sloppy Joe Barbecue, 121
  Stuffed Frankfurters, 123
  Swiss Salmon, 118
  Tacos, 125
  Tuna Cheese Buns, 124
  Tuna Cocktail for, 121
  Tuna Salad, 34
Saturated fats, 194
Sauce
  Custard, 161
  Golden Tartar, 106
Sauerkraut
  Confetti Salad, 56
  Reuben Sandwich Filling, 112
Sausage
  Pizza Muffins, 117
  Pizzas, 127
  Sandwiches, Marinated, 113
Scandinavian Egg Salad, 119

Seeds
  Five-Cup Snack Mix, 13
  Good Health Bars, 147
  Honey Nut Butter, 14
  Sunflower Refrigerator Cookies,
    139
  Sunflower Wheat Muffins, 87
  Super Chocolate Chip Cookies,
    141
  Zucchini Nut Bread, 84
Sherbet
  Cranberry Orange, 38
  Strawberry Buttermilk, 35
  Three Fruit, 35
Slaw, Vegetable, 31
Slim Jim Cheeseburger, 33
Slimmers' Deviled Eggs, 27
Sloppy Joe Barbecue Sandwiches,
    121
Snackers' Casseroles, 131
Snacker's Tomato Soup, 29
Soup
  Bean, Ready-to-Pour, 49
  Beef-Vegetable, 28
  Chicken Vegetable, 128
  Chilled Borscht, 49
  freezing individual portions, 29
  Gazpacho, 28
  Italian Vegetable, 129
  Low-Cal Borscht, 27
  Snacker's Tomato, 29
  Texas Vegetable Soup, 130
  Yogurt Cucumber, 30
Soybeans, 189
Spicy Lemon Prune Cake, 153
Spicy Nuts, 14
Spread(s)
  Chocolate Peanut, 162
  Party Tuna, 103
  Tuna Butter, 119
  Tuna Cocktail for Sandwiches,
    121
  Tuna-Cream Cheese, 103

Strawberry
  Angel Dessert, 98
  Buttermilk Sherbet, 35
  Dip, 97
  Fizz, 24
  Malt, Super, 94
Stuffed Frankfurters, 123
Succotash Salad, 53
Sugar-Coated cereals, 192
Sugars and syrups, 178, 192–93
Sunflower Refrigerator Cookies,
  139
Sunflower Wheat Muffins, 87
Super Chocolate Chip Cookies,
  141
Super Fruited Muffins, 85
Super Strawberry Malt, 94
Surprise Cloverleafs, 78
Swedish Apple Pudding, 160
Sweet Potato Pecan Pie, 156
Swiss Salmon Sandwiches, 118

Taco Filling, 125
Tacos, 125
Tartar Sauce, Golden, 106
Texas Vegetable Soup, 130
Three Fruit Sherbet, 35
Toffee, Corn Nut, 16
Tomato(es)
  Beef Vegetable Soup, 28
  Blue Cheese, 51
  Gazpacho, 28
  Ground Beef Mini-Meal, 132
  Hamburger Pizzas, 127
  Homemade Pizza Sauce, 126
  Italian Vegetable Soup, 129
  Marinated, 51
  Marinated Sausage Sandwiches,
    113
  Marinated Vegetables, 58
  Mediterranean Salad, 32
  Mixed Vegetable Relish, 60
  Parmesan Garden Salad Bowl,
    56

Poor Man's Caviar, 48
  Ready-to-Pour Bean Soup, 49
  Salsa, 52
  Sausage Pizzas, 127
  Snacker's Tomato Soup, 29
  Tacos, 125
  Texas Vegetable Soup, 130
  Vegetable Marinade, 52
Tomato Juice
  Garden, 47
  Mulled, 23
  Piquant, 48
Topping, Pineapple, 159
Torte, Apple, 99
Tortillas
  Easy Nachos, 104
  Sandwiches, Grilled, 105
Tropical Fruit Shake, 43
Tuna
  Butter, 119
  Cheese Buns, 124
  Cocktail for Sandwiches, 121
  -Cream Cheese Spread, 103
  Nibblers, 26
  Parmesan Dip, 102
  Salad Sandwiches, 34
  Spread, Party, 103
  -Vegetable Casserole, 133

U. S. Recommended Daily
  Allowance (U.S. RDA), 179,
  181

Vanilla Milk Shake, 96
Vegetable oils and shortenings,
  194–95
Vegetable protein, 189
Vegetables, 41–43, 47–60. See also
  Individual Vegetables
  Beef Vegetable Soup, 28
  Chicken Vegetable Soup, 128
  Confetti Sauerkraut Salad, 56
  Gazpacho, 28
  Ground Beef Mini-Meal, 132

Individual Chicken Casseroles, 134
Italian Chef's Salad Mix, 55
Italian Vegetable Soup, 129
Marinade, 52
Marinated, 58
Mediterranean Salad, 32
Mixed Vegetable Relish, 60
Mixed Vegetable Salad, 59
nutrients supplied by, 182–84
Orange and Yellow Salad, 59
Parmesan Garden Salad Bowl, 56
Poor Man's Caviar, 48
Salsa, 52
Slaw, 31
Succotash Salad, 53
Texas Vegetable Soup, 130
Tuna-Vegetable Casserole, 133
Vitamins, 7–8, 177
in cereal grains, 9, 190–92
in eggs, 190
in fortified breakfast cereals, 191–92
in fruits and vegetables, 41–43, 178, 182–83
in meat, 187–90
in milk, 184–85

Waffles
Frozen Wheat, 89
Water, 178–79
Wheat germ, 190–91
Country-Style Granola, 13
Four-Grain Bread, 66
Fruit Nut Balls, 15
Good Health Bars, 147
Honey Fruit Bread, 81
Honeyed Raisin Cookies, 141
Super Chocolate Chip Cookies, 141
Wheat Batter Bread, 73
Whole Wheat Protein Bread, 69
Zucchini Nut Bread, 84

Wheat Sunflower Muffins, 87
Wheat Waffles, Frozen, 89
White Bread, High Protein, 71
Whole Wheat
Batter Bread, 73
Bran Bread, 70
Bread, 67
Buns, 74
Buttermilk Bread, 68
Cinnamon Rolls, 76
Pecan Rolls, 77
Protein Bread, 69
Sweet Roll Dough, 75
Wintertime Minted Fruit Cup, 37

Yeast breads and rolls, 65–80
Date Oatmeal Crescents, 79
Easy Oatmeal Bread, 74
English Oat Muffins, 80
Four Grain Bread, 66
High Protein White Bread, 71
Mixed Grain Raisin Bread, 65
Prune Bran Bread, 72
Surprise Cloverleafs, 87
Wheat Batter Bread, 73
Whole Wheat Bran Bread, 70
Whole Wheat Bread, 67
Whole Wheat Buns, 74
Whole Wheat Buttermilk Bread, 68
Whole Wheat Cinnamon Rolls, 76
Whole Wheat Pecan Rolls, 77
Whole Wheat Protein Bread, 69
Whole Wheat Sweet Roll Dough, 75
Yogurt, 186
Blueberry Sicles, 34
Cucumber Soup, 30
Dilled Cheese Dip, 100
French Onion Dip, 25
Fruit-Yogurt Combo, 61
Mediterranean Salad, 32

G 50

New-Fashioned Pumpkin Pie, 157
Peachy Cheese Dessert, 35
Pineapple Cheese-Stuffed Celery, 25
Raspberry Pops, 36
Spicy Yogurt with Peaches, 37
Strawberry Angel Dessert, 98
Strawberry Dip, 97

Zesty Cheese Dip, 26
Zippy Beef Dip, 102
Zucchini
Marinated Vegetables, 58
Mediterranean Salad, 32
Mixed Vegetable Relish, 60
Nut Bread, 84
Parmesan Garden Salad Bowl, 56

Variety is the key to good nutrition. Everyone should eat the minimum number of servings of each of the basic foods each day. Size of servings depends on the individual. The servings described on this chart are average adult servings. Young children and adults who are not active or who are dieting, should eat smaller servings. Adults and teen-agers who are active and/or still growing may eat larger servings and extra servings.

FRUITS AND VEGETABLES

Valuable chiefly for vitamins and minerals. They also supply carbohydrates (starch and sugar) and fiber.

Eat 3 or 4 (or more) servings daily. Count as 1 serving: ½ cup vegetable, fruit or fruit juice; or a portion as ordinarily served such as 1 medium apple, banana, orange or potato, half a medium grapefruit or cantaloupe, juice of 1 lemon.

• Every day, eat 1 good source, or 2 fair sources of vitamin C: *Good sources:* Grapefruit or grapefruit juice, orange or orange juice, cantaloupe, raw strawberries, papaya, guava, mango, broccoli, Brussels sprouts, green pepper, sweet red pepper. *Fair sources:* Honeydew melon, lemon, tangerine or tangerine juice, watermelon, asparagus tips, raw cabbage, collards, cress, kale, kohlrabi, mustard greens, potatoes and sweet potatoes cooked in the jacket, spinach, tomatoes or tomato juice, turnip greens.
• Every other day, eat 1 good source of vitamin A: dark-green or deep-yellow vegetables and fruits, namely, apricots, cantaloupe, mangos, persimmon, broccoli, carrots, chard, collards, cress, kale, pumpkin, spinach, sweet potatoes, turnip greens and, winter squash.

Note: If the food chosen for vitamin C is also a good source of vitamin A, the single serving will fill the need for both vitamins. Your remaining 2 or 3 servings may be any vegetable or fruit—including those valuable for vitamins A and C.

FATS AND OILS

Valuable for energy and for necessary fatty acids. They also provide some vitamins. Some fat each day should come from vegetable oils that supply polyunsaturated fatty acids. But most people should cut down on fat intake.